James W. Kimball

How to See Jesus with Fullness of Joy and Peace

James W. Kimball

How to See Jesus with Fullness of Joy and Peace

ISBN/EAN: 9783337225797

Printed in Europe, USA, Canada, Australia, Japan

Cover: Foto ©Lupo / pixelio.de

More available books at **www.hansebooks.com**

WITH

FULNESS OF JOY AND PEACE.

BY

JAMES WILLIAM KIMBALL,

AUTHOR OF "HEAVEN," "FRIENDLY WORDS WITH FELLOW PILGRIMS,"
"ENCOURAGEMENTS TO FAITH," "ORIENT," "AN INDEX
TO THE BIBLE," ETC.

PUBLISHED BY

HOWARD GANNETT,

52 BROMFIELD STREET, BOSTON.

1880.

INTRODUCTION.

"Sweet promptings unto kindest deeds
    Were in her very look;
We read her face, as one who reads
    A true and holy book;

"Alone unto our Father's will
    One thought hath reconciled;
That He whose love excelleth ours
    Hath taken home His child."

IN one of our New England towns dwelt a minister of Christ, whose one solicitude was, to preach the gospel to every member of his parish. His wife was like-minded. They were both walking in all the commandments and ordinances of the Lord blameless, and were honored of God with great usefulness.

Mrs. Emily T. G. was anxiously waiting for the promise of the Saviour: "He that loveth me shall be loved of my Father, and I will love him, and will manifest myself to him."

A friend put into her hand three little tracts, frank utterances of a heart happy in the love of Jesus. These heart-revealings moved her to communicate with the writer, and led to a correspondence which in part is here presented.

No apology is offered for the personalities permitted to remain. Said Rev. John Angell James, "If I have been of any considerable service to my people, it is owing very much to the habit of showing them my heart; of sharing with them the joys and sorrows with which God has fashioned my own life." We shall find apostolic precedent for this habit.

This, then, is a heart offering "from the heart to the heart" of those who are waiting for the promised manifestation of the Lord Jesus. John xiv. 21.

PREFACE TO NEW EDITION.

Kind words from many parts of our own and from other lands, gratefully acknowledging help in seeing Jesus, and increase even to fulness of joy and peace in believing, impel me to renew the issue of this little book.

21 SOMERSET STREET,
September 1, 1880.

CONTENTS.

		PAGE
I.	Longing to see Jesus	7
II.	The Earnest of the Spirit	13
III.	Unbelief not Modesty	31
IV.	God's Love	35
V.	God's Promises	44
VI.	Thanksgiving	53
VII.	Guidance	59
VIII.	Trial of Faith	70
IX.	God's Minute Care	77
X.	Looking to Jesus	81
XI.	Trials	88
XII.	Revived Faith	98
XIII.	Patient Waiting	105
XIV.	Faith's Power	109
XV.	Peaceful Love	119
XVI.	Real Prayer	129
XVII.	Barrenness	133
XVIII.	Jesus' Tenderness	138
XIX.	Weighing Evidence	144
XX.	Faith's Scale	150
XXI.	Faith's Discipline	155
XXII.	Frustrating Grace	161

XXIII. God's Part and Ours	166
XXIV. Perplexities	176
XXV. Realizing Jesus	184
XXVI. Completeness in Jesus	192
XXVII. Lessons	197
XXVIII. Aspiration	204
XXIX. Walking with God	210
XXX. Proving all Things	216
XXXI. Hope deferred	222
XXXII. Jesus only	229
XXXIII. Feed my Lambs	234
XXXIV. Hope	238
XXXV. Coming Victory	243
XXXVI. Peace	246

HOW TO SEE JESUS.

I.

LONGING TO SEE JESUS.

"Long did I toil, and knew no earthly rest;
　Far did I rove, and found no certain home;
At last I sought them in His sheltering breast
　Who opes His arms and bids the weary come;
With Him I found a home, a rest divine;
And I, since then, am His, and He is mine."

I THANK you heartily for your kind letter. It makes me very glad to know that Jesus accepts my endeavor, and permits me to be helpful to any of His beloved ones. Your frank comments on the little Tracts encourage me to tell you something of the exceeding goodness of God which led to the experience, and compelled my acknowledgment in the words of the Psalmist: "I delight to do Thy will, O my God; yea, Thy law is within my heart. I have not hid Thy righteousness within my heart; I have declared Thy faithfulness and Thy salvation." It may be that the dear Lord will use this declaration of His faithfulness to encourage and strengthen you.

It was on the 25th April, 1831, I first found God real. From that day He has permitted no interruption to the friendship then so royally tendered; no cloud to come between my soul and Himself, the Sun of Righteousness. From my birth, and from my surroundings, it was a matter of course that I should receive line upon line, and precept upon precept; and yet, at nineteen, I had never once seen Jesus, nor the way to Him. I had been told in almost every form of utterance current in those days, that I ought to give my heart to Jesus. But, alas! it was assumed by those who said it, that I knew what it was to give my heart to Him; a most mistaken assumption. No doubt it was my own fault that I did not know. I wonder at my ignorance. But I wonder yet more, that those who really longed to lead inquiring souls to Jesus, should unconsciously leave me so utterly ignorant of the way. There was, however, this advantage in being so left; I was compelled to appeal to Him alone, for instruction. I cried unto the Lord. I sought Him with my whole heart. I entreated Him to reveal Himself unto me, as the willing and able Saviour I could not but know Him to be. For a year or more He had been drawing me on to this serious, and now, at length, to this undivided search for Him. Now, truly, He bowed the heavens and came down. He put darkness under His feet. My darkness He scattered. At the brightness that was before Him, His thick clouds passed, and His presence stood confessed.

As I came down from the place of prayer, I found myself talking with the Holy Ghost, as with an honored, revered, beloved, self-invited Guest, who so won upon my heart that I could not but entreat Him not to leave me; entreat Him to be my perpetual Guest.

Well might the poet sing:—

> "Like Morning, when her early breeze
> Breaks up the surface of the seas,
> That in their furrows dark with night,
> Her hand may sow the seeds of light,—
> Thy grace can send its breathings o'er
> The spirit dark and lost before;
> And, freshening all its depths, prepare
> For truth divine to enter there."

So I found it. And thus enriched, I hasten to assure you that a like bounteous grace awaits your riper need.

No sooner had I thus received the promise of the Father, the indwelling Comforter, than I became vividly aware of strange differences in those who professed to be followers and servants of Jesus. All assented to the truths which were to be believed about Him; all made confession of their faith in Him, and in much the same words; but to most, He did not seem to be a person, and a friend. It was as though they had heard of Him by the hearing of the ear, but did not really know Him; did not conceive that He is knowable. I congratulate you that our dear Lord has filled you with the conception and the desire to know Him intimately. At the time I speak of, and long after, I was much perplexed over the question, What is this difference in Christians? After a while our Lord's own words began to shed light upon it: "Many are called but few are chosen." Jesus said, "Except ye eat my flesh and drink my blood ye have no life in you;" they said, "This is an hard saying; who can hear it?" Again it is said: "From that time many of His disciples went back and walked no more with Him." When Jesus was arrested by the soldiers, "then all the disciples forsook Him, and fled."

To my apprehension it appears, from your own words, that you are of those who are both called and chosen of God, to be favored with His peculiar friendship. For this you hunger and thirst. You are not, therefore, a way-side hearer. The good seed has not fallen on stony ground, where there is not much depth of earth. Neither do I believe the cares of this world or the deceitfulness of riches choke the word. Your difficulty is of quite another kind. You are timid, and of a fearful heart. Here is a message of cheer for you: "Say to them that are of a fearful heart, Be strong, fear not, your God will come and save you."

Here is a song made ready to your need by another sister in Christ:—

> "I cannot think but God must know
> About the thing I long for so;
> I know He is so good, so kind,
> I cannot think but He will find
> Some way to help, some way to show
> Me to the thing I long for so."

Cherish the thought, dear friend. I am sure you will not be disappointed. You know Jesus says, "Blessed are they that hunger and thirst after righteousness." You are therefore blessed. You have received, in that hunger and thirst, a sure earnest of His promised manifestation of Himself to you. What if the vision tarry? You have but to wait on the Lord. "He that shall come will come, and will not tarry." I cannot, with some, be swift to say, that all may come at once into full possession of that liberty and joy in Christ which you so earnestly desire. In the beginning of my new life I might have thought so. But, alas! the evidence was soon forced upon me that the desire of many is neither deep nor strong. Jesus says of such, "they receive the word with joy, but have not root; they endure for a while, but when tribulation or persecution arise because of the word, they are offended." Assuredly all are invited, but all do not choose to come. They are not ready to serve the Lord with what costs them something. They are not prepared to honor Him with a self-consecration which may involve a risk. Of such as desire intimate association with

Him, He inquires, Are ye able to drink of my cup, and to be baptized with my baptism? They reply, We are able; but they know not what they speak; they have not carefully weighed what may be implied in it. Consciously or unconsciously they shrink; such shrinking is unbelief; they dare not commit their way unto the Lord. They have not sufficiently studied what He has said and done and suffered in their behalf; and therefore it is that they have not been fully persuaded of His love. They gain no clear vision, because it is only with the mind they seek Him. The heart must be aroused. "Then ye shall seek me, and find me, when ye shall search for me with all your heart."

II.

THE EARNEST OF THE SPIRIT.

> "O Love Divine! that stooped to share
> Our sharpest pang, our bitterest tear,
> On Thee we cast each earthborn care,
> We smile at pain when Thou art near.
>
> "Though long the weary way we tread,
> And sorrow crown each lingering year,
> No path we shun, no darkness dread,
> Our hearts still whispering, Thou art near.
>
> "On Thee we fling our burdening woe,
> O Love Divine, forever dear;
> Content to suffer while we know,
> Living or dying, Thou art near!"

DEAR Doctor T. H. Skinner, in his "Religion of the Bible," says: "There are three kinds of religion among those who call themselves Christians. Of one kind it were well if the world were destitute. Excepting by the observance of religious rites and solemnities, it does not distinguish the lives of those who practice it from the lives of irreligious men. It is the form of godliness without its power; the religion which would serve at the same time two masters, would join light and darkness, Christ and Belial, believers and unbelievers together.

"There is another kind of religion which has been called the middle path of Christianity. It is the religion manifestly of the generality of those who are considered Christians. It embraces, besides a profession and the observance of ordinances, a belief of the doctrines, and an irreprehensible outward conformity to the duties of the Gospel. But it falls short of the privileges of the Gospel; not including those lively hopes and anticipations, those holy joys and sorrows, that sensible intercourse and fellowship with God and Christ, that enrapturing communion with the Holy Spirit, that vivid and permanent earnest and assurance of Heaven, which the Gospel warrants and encourages in every believer.

"A third kind of religion is that which does include these peculiar experiences. We would designate it Spiritual Religion."

The Doctor goes on to state at some length what would satisfy Christians of this class; and especially this: "There must be a feeling of the Divine presence. If the light of God's countenance ceases at any time to shine upon the soul, the darkness which then covers it no outward prosperity can dispel; its sorrows nothing can alleviate. No loveliness, no excellence remains, when the heart cannot taste the excellency of the knowledge of Christ."

It is plain to me that He has called you into this class. You long for the vision of Christ; for the heart-sight and realization of Him as your present loving Lord. You know that some Christians are thus honored, and grieve that is not your happy experience; but you question if it is for you. I, on the other hand, am persuaded that a careful survey of the evidence Divinely provided must convince you that the happy experience you crave is freely tendered you. That your earnest desire for the loving and loved friendship of Jesus is a sure token of this. It is the earnest of the Spirit, 2 Cor. i. 22, and v. 5; Eph. i. 14. From the beginning God has sought the confidence and love of His creatures. He planted a garden in Eden, and in it He placed Adam. Out of the ground He made to grow every tree that is pleasant to the sight and good for food. He might have furnished man with simple instincts only, as He did the animals, and in so doing secured an unthinking and uninterested conformity to His own will. For our happiness, not less than for His own glory, He chose to create man in His own image; that is, with freedom of will; with power to love and to hate, to perceive, reflect, compare, contrast, to choose, refuse, or to coöperate; in short to live, in a measure more or less extended, on His own plane; that is, in friendship, fellowship, and sympathy with God.

The perception of God's design and desire survives the disastrous result of Satan's plot to destroy all such Divine and human friendship. If Cain was a rebel, Abel was loyal. After Abel came Enoch, who walked with God, and won the sweet assurance that he pleased God. Need I remind you of Abraham, Moses, Samuel, Elijah, Daniel, Paul, John, and a glorious cloud of witnesses whose record attests the reality of this exalted fellowship? To them God was entirely real and accessible. They knew and talked with Him as a friend. They aimed to please Him, and did not find Him hard to please. When they erred, He was very pitiful and of tender mercy. True these were exceptions to the multitude, but all were invited and commanded. Those who refused, did so on their own election. In the infancy of the race God entered into covenant with Abraham, for Himself and for all believers. The law given at Sinai contained no revocation of that covenant. Nay, it demanded the embodiment in daily life of the faith on which that covenant was based.

"Thou shalt love the Lord thy God with all thy heart, soul, mind, and strength," presupposes the closest intimacy with God in Christ. Without this, compliance is simply and utterly impossible.

I am sure, my dear friend, you must have remarked the growing conviction that average "Christian living" is unsatisfactory. It does not and cannot meet the need of earnest souls. The great majority of those who come to the table of our Lord own that Jesus is not realized as that personal present friend He declares Himself to be. To such, on their own confession, "prayer seems mere words in the air; a feeble and disheartened groping in the dark." It is infinitely short of what Jesus promises: namely, 1st. Forgiveness of sins, and freedom from condemnation. 1 John i. 7, 9; Rom. viii. 1. 2d. Deliverance from the law. Rom. vi. 14, and viii. 2. 3d. Sonship. Rom. viii. 14–16. 4th. Fellowship. Rom. viii. 17; 1 John i. 3. 5th. Holiness. Luke i. 74, 75; Rom. vi. 19, 22; Heb. xii. 10. 6th. Oneness with Christ. Rom. vi. 4, 6, 8; Rom. viii. 9; Gal. ii. 20. 7th. His peace. John xiv. 27. 8th. Indwelling and guidance of the Comforter. John xiv. 16, 17, 18, 26; John xvi. 13–15. 9th. Victory. John xi. 25, 26; 1 Cor. xv. 57. Here is the provision, Divinely made, that Christ may dwell in your heart by faith; that you may comprehend His love, which passeth knowledge, and be filled with all the fullness of God. Eph. iii. 17–19.

In some vague, purposeless, and unsatisfactory recognition, it is generally admitted that this ought to be the experience of all believers. It could not well be denied. The Word of God has too many and too precise commands and assurances to permit the denial. By a limited number it is positively affirmed to be the one Christian experience proper to all; and recognized by the godly in every age. A continuous, stable, intelligent, and unwavering faith, is felt to be the only faith that honors God. Illustrations of such faith are not wanting in our times. President Edwards and his wife, Brainard, Martyn, Dr. Payson, Muller, Josiah Bissell, Dr.

Wm. Goodell, Moody, and not a few less conspicuous Christians, are well known as exemplifying this life of continuous, conscious communion and fellowship with our Lord. It is a life of supreme and unquestionable devotion to Christ and His Church; an intelligent and total surrender and gift of one's self to Christ, not alone to do, but also to be, and to suffer, everything He pleases; and this in all the hours and activities of common every-day life, as completely as in the church, and on the Sabbath. It is a simple, intelligent, hearty, matter of fact reception of the Comforter, the Holy Ghost, on the simple word of the Lord Jesus, as a constant, permanent, and most loving guest, adviser, guide, and friend. It is a heart-reception, that knows no unreality, and requires no sensuous impression. The Holy Ghost once thus received, is Christ in you; Christ made real; a reality incomparably transcending all material and all scientific illustration; a perennial fountain of joy; a deep well of peace; including the "persuasion that neither death, nor life, nor angels, nor principalities, nor powers, nor things present, nor things to come, nor height, nor depth, nor any other creature, shall be able to separate you from the love of God, which is in Christ Jesus your Lord."

This life and experience is found in the children of God in every variety of circumstances; in those of few as well as in those of many talents; the learned and the unlearned. To expect an equally intelligent and properly guarded account of their actual gain, from each of these, would therefore be unreasonable. We can sometimes accept and profit by a statement of facts when we can neither profit by nor accept an attempted interpretation of the facts. Thus, a most happy deliverance from spiritual bondage, actually received, might be very inaccurately reported, or mistaken for something more and other than the fact. Undoubtedly our Lord's oft repeated admonition, "If thou canst believe; all things are possible to him that believeth;" was designed to call attention to that one special impediment, ever in our way, unbelief. But there are other hindrances, which may not be ignored. Thus, for example: "Justice and judgment are the habitation of Thy home; mercy and truth shall go before Thy face." The first of these characteristics of our Heavenly Father are as carefully to be remembered as the other. And yet, dear friend, because of the present impossibility of bringing your daily life at once into entire conformity with the Divine standard, to conclude that your Father cannot regard you as a beloved child, is grievously to misjudge Him. If this were so, every conscientious Christian might well despair. The Gospel is indeed the glorious Gospel of the blessed God for penitent sinners. Our beloved brother Paul says: "And the grace"—that is, the undeserved favor— "of our Lord was exceeding abundant with faith and love which is in Christ Jesus. This is a faithful saying, and worthy of all acceptation, that Christ Jesus came into the world to save sinners, of whom I am chief." And so when a disciple of Jesus is enabled to receive his Lord as his Immanuel, his salvation as a present and complete salvation, and to find the yoke of Christ easy and his burden light, is it any wonder if he, unaccustomed to use language with metaphysical exactitude, should seem to overstate what he has received? Let no statement of this kind dishearten you. Appeal from and concerning it, to your loving Lord and He will surely guide you; for so He promises.

So different is the free and joyous life of many a witness from the life he before groaned under, you cannot wonder if he hastens to conclude that "Christ is doing everything for him." For so indeed He is; though not in contravention of His own declaration that "He works in us to will and to do of His own good pleasure."

But to some who cordially recognize a life in the very sunlight of the Divine love, as not an unprecedented thing, it seems a question if there be any true and well-warranted Christian state which may properly be called the rest of faith; that peaceful and continuous assurance of Christ's intimate friendship and approving love, for which you sigh.

Alas! but too distinctly do I remember the gall and wormwood of an endless succession of abortive endeavors to live in sinless loyalty to Christ. Who can count the resolutions broken, or who portray the painful sense of shamelessness, amounting to audacity, in even presuming again to ask forgiveness, with no assurance of doing better? What but bitter waters could come of this? And this came of halting faith; lame for lack of realizing Jesus as the Lamb of God taking away the sins of the world by the sacrifice of himself. Nevertheless, though missed by not a few, there is a peaceful, as well as a joyous, knowledge of God. The declaration, "Thou wilt keep him in perfect peace whose mind is stayed on Thee, because he trusteth in Thee," is not the proclamation of a mere mathematical point, or of an equatorial line, whose existence may not be denied, but which cannot be actualized. It may not please God immediately to bestow so great a gift. Delay may be needed to free the believer from temptation to rob God, by assuming that his own right arm hath gotten him the victory. "What hast thou that thou didst not receive?" may be an ever-present and ever-needed reminder, designed to preclude all arrogance and self conceit; and it is not difficult to conceive of great advantage to be derived from schooling our strong natural preferences into cheerful acquiescence in the will of God.

Though forty years without a doubt of my sonship, and with the realization of Christ's presence and of His tender love never once suspended, somehow I missed that being "careful for nothing," to which He summons us. Like yourself, I was self-condemned that I was not "kept in perfect peace."

Like yourself, I had been taught, with much painstaking, the efficacy of Christ's atoning sacrifice. I knew that "the blood of Jesus Christ cleanseth from all sin." I had earnestly offered this full salvation to not a few, and yet, after all this, I had not myself fully appropriated it.

If you ask, "How is this to be accounted for?" I answer, I suspect the explanation to be, that I did not and could not at once receive the Word of God in utter simplicity. It came to me veiled and obscured in a cloud of human traditions and interpretations. Thus, when I read God's declaration of the efficacy of the blood of Jesus, that declaration was glossed with the suggestion, Take heed that you do not understand this literally, for though whatever the Lord says is true, in a general way, yet proper knowledge of yourself, and of your failings, should and will forbid you to believe that He cleanses you from all unrighteousness. For generations the prevailing teaching has been, that to be doubtful of our acceptance with God is on the whole safer, and less liable to mislead, than undoubting assurance. This is the verdict of average thought, belief, and experience. And on such experience doubtless it is as much as we have warrant to affirm. Those who live only, or chiefly in fear, must needs challenge a love which casts out all fear. They frankly own the imperfection of their love; it has perhaps not occurred to them to suspect that their fear may be not less imperfect, and therefore equally unacceptable to God. All this befits a round of mere thought about religion and its requirements, discerning no "life with Christ in God." By the mouth of the Beloved Disciple, He says to us, "Beloved, if our heart condemn us not, then have we confidence toward God." The intellect may condemn; judgment and conscience may condemn; because, tried before their tribunal, I am found a sinner against God, exceeding sinful. And yet, thanks be to God, I may love Him with all my heart, soul, mind, and strength; with a true and honest heart; and so may you. I may be loved by Him, most tenderly, and so may you, because so wondrous is the efficacy of the atoning sacrifice of Christ, that I am no longer under the law of Sinai. I have been taken into the grace of the Divine friendship, and so have you. Faulty as I know myself to be, my heart does not condemn me. I have confidence toward God through our Lord Jesus Christ. Both heart and mind appropriate the atonement as completely as the sunlight, air, and bread, as received and used for the life of the body. I am no more a stranger and foreigner, but a fellow citizen with the saints, and of the household of God. I begin to discern the mysterious fellowship which from the beginning of the world hath been hid in God, who created all things by Jesus Christ. I am strengthened with might by His spirit in the inner man. Christ dwells in my heart by faith. I am rooted and grounded in love, and so enabled to comprehend with all saints, what is the breadth, and length, and depth, and height, and to know the love of Christ which passeth knowledge.

This is a true account of the issues from an honest, earnest walking with God, the normal and promised victories resulting from persistent fighting the good fight of faith. Must we then conclude that those who miss these issues are neither honest or earnest? By no means. Many who are both honest and earnest have been cheated of their birthright. "It pleased the Father that in Christ should all fullness dwell;" also "that we might be filled with all the fullness of God."

Is not this Divine testimony corroborated by the facts of human life? How is it in that friendship between man and man, which God has made the type of His own? I am your friend. A very imperfect friend, and yet an honest friend. Is there any insuperable impediment to loving an honest friend, one who in mind and heart is devoted to your interests, because he is not perfect?

My own judgment is, that some of those whom the Lord has made very happy and restful in Him, mistake in thinking that their fellow Christians universally, irrespective of natural gifts, irrespective of education and training, human and divine, may, if earnestly urged, instantaneously appropriate their proffered key, enter their door, and enjoy their happy relations to God. Nevertheless, there is for such as can and do rightly receive Christ a deliverance from bondage. For it is written, "As many as received Him, to them gave He power to become the sons of God." "These things have I spoken unto you, that my joy might remain in you, and that your joy might be full." "Peace I leave with you; my peace I give unto you." He does not say that every Christian will accept what He so freely gives. He does not say that all who desire will do this. He does say, "Blessed are they that hunger and thirst, for they shall be filled."

No earnest, reverent Christian will, in express terms, question the Divine assurance: "Thou wilt keep him in perfect peace whose mind is stayed on Thee." Yet, in effect, not a few do make void this grace of God. From their own experience, and by the prevailing testimony of their fellow-professors, they are persuaded that the Christian life is a continuous personal race; a wrestling against principalities and powers; an unending struggle with the world, the flesh, and the devil; a striving in the seldom, if ever, intermittent agony of personal combat, which permits no laying down of anxious solicitude for the result; which endless struggling, disguise it as we may, is torment. Through fear of defeat, if not of death, such are all their lifetime subject to bondage.

I might ask of those who thus mistakenly insist, Does this anxious solicitude comport with perfect peace? Does it comport with the assurance that Jesus "took part of flesh and blood, that through death He might destroy him that had the power of death, that is, the devil; and deliver them who, through fear of death, were all their lifetime subject to bondage?" I might ask, which horn of the dilemma will you choose? That there is no perfect peace, no adequate deliverance, no peace-pervading, serene, uninterrupted heart-union with Jesus, this side of death? that Jesus failed in his atoning mission? or that our Lord mocks us with deceiving words He never intended to have a real meaning?

No doubt our day has its peculiar antagonisms to the exercise of simple faith. Each age in the world's history has had its own. But "an obstacle," as has been well said, "is a thing to be surmounted." Were it not so, our beloved brother Paul might be charged with uttering idle words, with tendering an unmeaning ascription, when he cried out, "Thanks be to God, who giveth us the victory through our Lord Jesus Christ;" and no less when he added, "Therefore, my beloved brethren, be ye steadfast, unmovable, always abounding in the work of the Lord, forasmuch as ye know that your labor is not in vain in the Lord." If the victory is delayed, it is the part of loving confidence and trust in our Lord, to own that there must be adequate reasons, and to search diligently and patiently for them. It is not the part of faith, but of unworthy, guilty unbelief, to assume that there is never in the Christian life a victory that raises the devoted child of God above a ceaseless fight over the self-same ground. Will either of us venture to assert, that there are no fields in this great contest, which being fought and won, may thenceforth be possessed for Christ, requiring not to be fought again? Does the true life in Christ record no permanent victories? Has our Lord no happy, joyous victors under His banner, or only one or two in a generation? Is the new life, the risen life in Christ, only an endless chain of ever recurring temptation, sinning and repenting, in the self-same ruts? Nay, more, and worse; is Christ in us, not only over and over again, but always defeated?

Such surely is not the testimony of that great cloud of witnesses summoned to testify in the eleventh of Hebrews. Such is not the testimony of the Apostle Paul, of Peter, or of John. Such could not be the testimony of any in our own day who are followers of God as dear children; who walk in love, as Christ also hath loved us. To such He says: "As the Father hath loved me, so have I loved you." Are these unmeaning words? Do they permit you to affirm, Jesus will not give me the fullness of love, and of realization of His love, I crave? No indeed!

But here is the solution: There is an indefinite amount of duty-service, up to which men are driven by the thunders of Sinai, and by the echoes of conscience, a service fitly responding to the temper and spirit of our times. Who is prepared with Paul and John for total consecration, and for implicit and utter trust? Who dare appeal to God to forbid and to exclude all glorying save in the cross of Christ? Who courts crucifixion with Christ? Who knows himself dead to the world, and hid with Christ in God? That way of living is as free as at any former time. Alas! the sacrifice is ready for Mammon, for Moloch, for Bacchus, for Minerva, it may be; for all the gods of the heathen, and for any idol. Our daily papers do but swell the catalogue of victims at such shrines. But a living sacrifice on the altar of Christ challenges belief. Ministers at His altar even are doubtful if there be in our day any veritable living sacrifice, holy, acceptable unto God. They find the maimed, the halt, and the blind, that is, followers of Christ who confess that they are not following Him fully, who do not claim that they are even attempting a total consecration; who deny the possibility of faithful following, and permit the doubt of such to weigh against the testimony of Peter (2 Peter i. 1–11), of Paul (2 Tim. iv. 7, 8), and of John (1 John i. 3, 7, 9).

To such, our Lord's reply is: "Whosoever he be of you that forsaketh not all that he hath, he cannot be my disciple." There is a secret of the Lord. He does not reveal Himself to those who give Him but a partial trust. The disappointment of such is not to be taken as proof that Jesus will not manifest Himself to those who love Him and keep His words. To those who take Jesus at His word, the Comforter does come. In them He dwells. He shows them the things of God and of Christ, and leads them into all truth. His presence dissolves all fears, swallows up all solicitudes, and is the earnest and foretaste of Heaven. Speak then to Jesus the language of love; read, aye and shout to Him the 23d Psalm, the 34th, the 62d, the 103d, the 112th, and the 145th, and see to it that your heart fills, pervades, and overflows in these heartlife words. Throw your heart into these and into such like utterances a hundred times a day.

Only believe, that much as you desire this most intimate, loving, peaceful, conscious friendship with our beloved Lord, He much more desires it; and you will have it. What if He keeps you waiting for a time? Did He not test the Syrophenician woman? And was it not to exalt her to honor before the endless ages? "It is good that a man should both hope and quietly wait for the salvation of the Lord;" that is, wait in the quietness of loving trust for this fullness of salvation.

Faith fearlessly affirms that Jesus has manifold and admirable reasons for divers dealings with the disciples who entreat to be admitted to His most intimate fellowship.

"Lord, Thou wilt love me. Wilt Thou not?
Beshrew that not:
It was my sin begot

That question first.   Yes, Lord, Thou wilt:
Thy blood was spilt
To wash away my guilt.
Lord, I will love Thee.   Shall I not?
Beshrew that not."

III.

UNBELIEF NOT MODESTY.

> "Yield to the Lord, with simple heart,
> All that thou hast, and all thou art;
> Renounce all strength but strength divine,
> And peace shall be forever thine;
> Behold the paths the saints have trod,
> The paths which led them home to God."

I CANNOT quite feel satisfied to let you alone this morning. I feel about you as Goodwill, in Bunyan, felt about Christian. He wanted to lay hold on him and pull him within the gate, before the archers across the way could wound him with their sharp arrows. Naturally modest and reticent, you have unconsciously nursed the idea that it would be presumptuous in you promptly to believe, when you give yourself to Jesus, that He actually and warmly receives you. Satan does not spare to assail you with disheartening suggestions. Thus: "God never has been real to you; He is not now; you cannot see Him, hear Him, nor touch Him. No man has seen Him; no man can. Those who pretend it, as you well know, often give least evidence of it in their lives. Job did not know where to find Him; though God himself told me, Job was a perfect and upright man, one that feared God and eschewed evil, and there was none like him. If God hid Himself from Job, why should He show Himself to you?" To all this your safest answer is: "Get thee behind me, Satan." "When Thou saidst unto me, 'Seek ye my face,' my heart said unto Thee: 'Thy face, Lord, will I seek.' Hide not Thy face from me. The pure in heart shall see God; for Thou hast said it. Lord, make me pure in heart, for I am fully purposed that I will see Thee." To this His answer ever is, "According to thy faith be it unto thee." It remains for you to speak to Him as to a real, a present, and a loving Friend; to open your whole heart to Him. Take up His promises which warrant such speech with Him. Take one by one, and plead it. Insist with unshrinking pertinacity, that you have His warrant for so doing, and that you never will cease pressing for this favor till He grants it. Has He ever forfeited His word? Will He begin with you? No; for He abideth faithful. He cannot deny Himself. Take care to say only what you mean; to use only the words which clearly express your meaning. Above all, see to it that what you say is your heart's utterance. "Trust in Him at all times, ye people, pour out your heart before Him."

Now I must not speak pityingly of your holding back, nor for a moment consent to regard it as proper modesty. For, admitting as quite true all that you can allege of your undeserving and ill deserving, I must demand of you, How dare you make that a pretext for discrediting the solemn, earnest, heart-moving asseveration of your Lord, that He will and does receive you? This is your particular and preëminent sin, — this unbelief of his specific promises, — which you are to confess to God; imploring Him to conquer what you find too strong for you. Hate this unbelief in God's love. You do not begin to realize how sinful and how hurtful it is. You do not conceive what an indignity it puts upon God.

You, perhaps, know some poor, degraded, ignorant person whom it is in your heart to benefit and elevate. You exert yourself to the utmost to do him good. Your reward is, that your good-will is declined, disbelieved, ignored. You are told, we will suppose, by the object of your kind endeavors, that he could not possibly do so immodest a thing as to believe that you mean your kindness for him. He prefers to believe that you intend kindness to mankind in general. How would you feel under such a repulse? Would the miscalled modesty of it mend the matter, or save your wounded feelings?

You have a chronic habit of doubting: do you find anything good in it, anything lovely, or to be desired? Hate it, spurn it, as the vilest thing you know; and protest —

> "I will believe! I now believe!
> I can hold out no more;

> I sink, by dying love compelled,
> And own Thee conqueror."

I had a call a year ago from a young lady who came to our city to get a school. I gave her a note to the chairman of the school committee; but there was no vacancy. I said to her: Now I want you to promise me this; that you will make a new, and a great deal more thorough gift of yourself to the Lord; and that you will especially commit this matter of the school unqualifiedly to Him. Do that and He will give you a school, if it is best, in the best time.

"She thought God helped those who helped themselves."

So He does; but there is no way in which you can so effectively help yourself as in doing just this. She promised; and she did it; and the Lord took up my pledge, and gave her a school at the end of a year, or less; and gave her most profitable preparatory discipline in the mean time. "If thou canst believe, all things are possible to him that believeth." Only give and commit all that you have, and are, and hope, and wish, and fear, to Him; that is all. Only receive the Holy Ghost. Only offer Him sincerely and cordially the hospitalities of your heart; prepare Him room, and He will dwell with you, and do all.

IV.

GOD'S LOVE.

> "Like a cradle rocking, rocking,
>   Silent, peaceful, to and fro,
> Like a mother's sweet looks dropping
>   On the little face below,
> Hangs the green earth, swinging, turning,
>   Jarless, noiseless, safe and slow;
> Falls the light of God's face bending
>   Down, and watching us below."

WHEN I was converted, I hardly dared to go to sleep, lest I should lose ground. But then I bethought me — I ought rather to say, the Lord suggested — that I should rest in His love. And so I said to him: "Lord Jesus, I have fought till I can fight no longer; I cannot keep myself; let me lay my head upon Thy bosom." And He did. And I slept — oh, so sweetly! I praised Him in my dreams, and waked with a song of praise on my lips and in my heart. When I went to my chamber to pray, I said, Now if my father were in the adjoining room, though I could not see him for the partition between us, I could know him to be there, and by raising my voice I could make him hear me. Well Jesus is here. I cannot see Him through this veil of flesh, but I know absolutely that He is here. I have no need to raise my voice, for He can hear the lowest whisper. Dear Jesus, I speak to Thee. I will tell Thee all my heart. Holy Spirit, guide me, that I may speak what thou wouldst have me. Make intercession within me. I entreat that my prayer may be Thy prayer. And then I turned to my Heavenly Father and asked Him if he would redeem the pledge of His Son. John xiv. 13, 14. I never have any confusion about Father, Son, and Holy Ghost. It is all just as I would have it. It makes our position so strong; our argument so irresistible. The Spirit originates the prayer; the blessed Saviour takes it up and advocates it; the Father gladly grants what is so acceptably presented. I often tell Him, He cannot say nay to His only begotten and well beloved Son, who is also my well beloved Lord.

You say, "If I could only learn to connect God with everything I hear and see."

Cherish that wish, and He will establish the connection for you. "If a man love me," said Jesus, "he will keep my words; and my Father will love him; and we will come unto him, and make our abode with him." Accustom yourself to the recognition of His having actually done that for you. The Holy Ghost, the Comforter, dwells with you, and in you. Do not ask, "How can these things be?" It is true because Jesus declared it should be so. Be sure that from the moment of your conversion, the Holy Ghost charged Himself with your education. And He makes no mistakes. He knows to a day, to an hour, when to put us upon this, that, and the other study. He knows what text books I need and provides them for me. I had Fenélon, for example, put into my hands at the fitting moment, so obviously, that a hand reached down from heaven could not more surely have verified His interposition. Of course you have your personal cares, your family cares, your peculiar cares as a pastor's wife. Take each and every one of them from the Lord. Take a headache from Him; take broken china from Him; take rainy Mondays from Him; take rainy church-meeting-nights from Him. It is wonderful how the habit of taking everything from Him, turns everything into a blessing. All things do work together for good to them that love God. I have proved it true thousands of times.

How natural is your expression, "I thought I was to be blamed because I was where I was. I have felt that if I had done differently, been more in earnest, had had more faith, prayed more, I should have been a more useful Christian."

All of which is true enough, in a way, but it overlooks what was to have secured all this to you; namely, just that overlooked, unappreciated, simple faith in your Father, Redeemer, Sanctifier.

I have never been more deeply touched than in the discovery of our Lord's using one of my faults to teach me the blessed lesson of humility. Now I was culpable, for my fault, of course; but, so far as I am able to judge, nothing in the world could have been so useful to me as being left to commit the fault, and to see my Lord using it to impart His lesson. Sometimes it has been an error too contemptibly little to be worth mentioning; and yet, so wonderful is the Divine alchemy, that that little, pitiful, nameless fault, in the hands of the infinitely wise and infinitely loving One, has been of a healing efficacy never to be forgotten. Consider that our God takes us just as we are, to make us just what He would have us be. Were this not so, our sufficiency would not be of God. 2 Cor. iii. 5. Our redemption from sin would not be wholly His work. Consider, if God were to make no use of our faults, for the disciplining and development of our souls, how large a part of all we have and are would be as it were without His province. Now you have only to remind yourself of Jesus' own gracious assurance, " I came not to call the righteous but sinners to repentance," to feel sure that his foresight and providence, all through the days of our impenitence even, were laying the foundation for the polished shaft He means to set up in the New Jerusalem. Is it not glorious to discern that even sin is so completely under the control of our Almighty Friend, that He can, not only limit its scope, but absolutely overrule it, so as that we shall be more capable of appreciating and of commending His love than if we had never sinned?

If this seems inadmissible, I leave it for those to settle who can show a better account of the matter. I fall back upon the unquestionable affirmation, God does, by the discipline of trials, brought upon us by our sins, qualify us to be helpful to sinners, as we could be qualified in no other way, so far as mind of man can see. You, at any rate, can "go on quietly to the end of your days," assured that God has so overruled your sins as that by the sin and the discipline, you have been fitted to pity, save, and build up in the faith those who have in like manner sinned. Suppose you had never sinned, had never been forgiven and rescued from the sins and their consequences; is it apparent how you could be touched with the feeling of the infirmities of those whom you are commissioned to save?

Your fear to apply endearing epithets to Jesus reminds me, comparing great things with small, of the boy who was not to go into the water until he had learned to swim. You starve your heart by withholding its proper food, and then wonder that it aches with hollow hunger. There never was a truer maxim than that familiarly used by the children: "Be thankful for little; that is the way to get more." You are surely sensible that Jesus has done something for you. Can you conceive of its being otherwise than agreeable to Him, that you should say, "Dear Jesus, I thank thee?" And when you have said that a few times it will sound so sweetly in your own ear, and so win upon you with its sweetness, that before you are well aware you will find yourself whispering, "Sweet Jesus, precious Jesus, beloved Saviour, light of my eyes, joy of my heart, comfort of my soul!" Be not faithless but believing.

"If you had allowed yourself more freedom of language towards Him, perhaps" —

No, no, no! There is no perhaps about it. You must learn to blot out that word, along with the word "discouraged." "If a man love me, he will keep my words," etc. You have kept His words.

"Not perfectly."

No, not perfectly. Jesus did not say "perfectly." You have kept them just as He knew you would keep them, when He uttered those words. And His Father, my Father, your Father, does love you, and has made His abode with you. And you must not think it is modest in you to doubt it. It is something not so innocent as modesty; it is unbelief. Imagine some other person coming to you, the pastor's wife, and telling her story; just your own story, word for word. Would you send her away uncomforted because she was only a penitent sinner? Because she had not loved perfectly?

I am glad you have abjured an endless round of self-bemoaning confessions. We are bound to get forgiveness, as well as bound to ask it. We are bound to believe 1 John i. 9. In regard to not feeling your sins as committed against God; that goes along with the habit you deplore, of not connecting everything with God. Establish that habit and the other will follow inevitably.

I did know when I proposed that you should refrain from petition and confine yourself for a week to thanksgiving, that you would think it very hard. And why? I once felt very much the same. It seemed to me that I was so great a sinner, and so weak withal, that it would never do to stop praying for myself, lest I should be swept right away from my new found Friend. I found out that this was pure unbelief; want of confidence in my Lord; and not that alone, but a mistaken idea that I was keeping myself. I wished you to make the same discovery. Therefore it was I proposed to you to ask no petitions for yourself, but keep to praise for a week. "Underneath" you, my dear friend, "are the everlasting arms." And you need have no fear that Jesus will withdraw them. Have you forgotten Isaiah xlix. 15? He will never, never, never leave thee nor forsake thee. I was talking yesterday with Rev. Dr. W. of the views of a mutual friend who makes growing in grace identical with a growing agony in prayer, and we agreed that the true place for agony is in coming into right relations with God; for example, in trying (according to Col. i. 10) to please God in all things; in agonizing endeavors to put away all that I have reason to think may be displeasing to Him.

But having adopted the plan of pleasing Him in all things as the one aim of my life, then I am set free from agony, as the rule; "the law of the spirit of life in Christ Jesus hath set me free from the law of sin and death;" and I may serenely rejoice in the contemplation of His attributes; or I may engage in any benevolent endeavor no less calmly; or I may turn from prayer to praise securely, knowing His own assurance, that "Whoso offereth praise glorifieth God." Make the case your own, now. Suppose you had a child so grateful to you for all your kindness, as to be quite drawn off from all thought of its wants; forgetful, even, for the time, how great its ignorance, and how many its faults. Think you you could leave that child while thus oblivious, and from such a cause, to come to any grief? One of your closing remarks touches me deeply. You say, "You are better acquainted with the Master than I am; won't you ask Him to keep me from growing careless and indifferent again?" Why, my beloved sister, how little you do Him justice. I have indeed already prayed for you with all the earnestness of my soul. But who prompted me so to pray for you? The Master Himself. And yet you want me to stir Him up to love and care for you. O thou of little faith! Do you think you know what a tender mother's love for her infant is? I have no doubt you do. But that is as nothing in comparison with His love for thee. But I am not impatient with you; I have good, blessed, glorious hopes for you. You are going to become strong in the Lord. You will never "become careless and indifferent again." Indeed, those words have not expressed the truth about you. You were not careless, but despondent. You intermitted exertion, because, not having right ideas of the way, you were hopeless. But now you are beginning to know the way, you will find it so alluring, I do not think you could be tempted to turn aside from it. Only renew the consecration of yourself to Jesus, very frequently, and very heartily, and you will have no occasion to "deplore the temptations of the world," as we hear so many do. You will be so filled and satisfied with the company of Jesus that you could no more go back to the world than you could go back to the toys of your babyhood. Let me animate you with the assurance that our Lord is well pleased to have you cherish great expectations from His munificence. You never can exceed — nay, you never can begin to imagine — all He is willing and exceedingly desirous to do for you: "Behold I have graven thee upon the palms of my hands." Do believe His love. I assure you from experience a thousand times renewed, it is ever enduring, infinitely manifold, and always seeking you. Do not say, or think, with the Assyrian lord: "If the Lord should make windows in Heaven, then might this thing be." The windows are already made, and open.

V.

GOD'S PROMISES.

> " Then my soul, in every strait,
> To thy Father come, and wait;
> He will answer every prayer,
> God is present everywhere."

YOU ask, How can I know that I do get forgiveness?

I answer: In 1833 our Father — yours and mine — put into my hands a little book of Robert Philip, entitled, "Communion with God." In it is a chapter, "The Promises of God to the Prayerful, the Real Answers to Prayer." This idea was then new to me. He enabled me to embrace it. I believe He will enable you to do the same. It is thus Jesus is seen; thus He manifests Himself; not to the eye, the ear, not to the mind even, so much as to the heart. No eye can compare with the heart's eye. You know how it is between thee and me. If you have my promise of something to be done for you, suppose next Tuesday, your faith receives that thing as sure. You have your Father's promise, " If we confess our sins, He is faithful and just to forgive us our sins, and to cleanse us from all unrighteousness." Is not this promise absolute?

You reply: "Ah, but it is qualified by my confessing. And how can I be sure that my confession comes within God's meaning?"

Do you not remember that it was agreed between us, that we were to stop in our inquiries at the margin of consciousness? There is a limit to all justifiable doubting. If, after careful, thoughtful self-examination, it appears to you that you are sincerely sorry for your sin, then you are no longer at liberty to doubt, that as it appears to you, so it really is; in other words, you are sorry for your sin. You confess it sincerely; your confession is the confession implied and demanded by our Lord. There remains, therefore, only that you believe, entirely believe that He does forgive and cleanse you from all unrighteousness.

Observe this is not "working yourself up" to believe; "working yourself up" to a mysterious and equivocal "feeling." It is only an intelligent, earnest demand of a reasoning, believing soul, upon itself, to honor God by believing Him. Is that clear? If I had given you assurance that I would do you some great favor, would it be fanaticism, or any working upon the imagination (while thinking, "What Mr. K. has promised is too good to believe!"), for you to go and get my letter, saying within yourself, "Let me see; let me carefully read over just what he did say"? And when you had thus carefully re-read, would you not be saying, "Why, yes, he surely does say that, just that, and I may rejoice in the certainty; it is all so"?

I think it very likely it was Satan that said to you, "You don't know anything of such a religion as this." Or it may have been the natural reasoning of a heart perverted by sin. It is always difficult, not to say impossible, to apportion the blame due to Satan and to ourselves. But, without intending improperly to lessen your culpability, I may say, your feeble piety may and must be referred in part to the atmosphere into which you were born. Do you know the memoir of James Brainerd Taylor? Had you been a member of his family, or had you been one of his Bible class, when he was studying in New Haven, it might and probably would have made a very great difference. In the begining we are greatly dependent upon the piety of others. But you are not to make the vehemence of "Orient's" experience a model for yourself, nor a standard by which to condemn your own; for this, among other reasons: that she was to live but two years after her conversion; and our Lord saw fit to crowd a life's work into that brief space. I would not, if I might, aim to have you just like her. Your work is different. Let us accept the wholesome stimulus which such a seraphic life inspires, but do not let us pervert it into a discouragement. A race-horse would not be as useful in the furrows of common life as an animal of more moderate movement. I cannot have you apply to yourself such language as you use. It is inapplicable. It is not true that you intentionally "deceive any one." You "desire to lead a Christian life." In the beginning of my religious life it troubled me greatly when I found no glow of love, no depth of sorrow, etc., etc., — just what you charge upon yourself. At last it occurred to me to ask, what is in fact the true test of the reality of any sentiment, How much feeling must one have, in order to be sure that he has the right feeling? And the Lord made me see that the feeling which secured appropriate action, was right both in kind and in degree. Since then I have often illustrated it thus: Suppose I were to become a member of your family. There are opportunities every day, every hour in the day, to act the part of a true friend; ten thousand little minute opportunities of being swayed by love to you. No great thing to be done; no demand for vehement feeling, or emotion of any kind; nothing to arrest the attention of others, only that often unconscious regulating of words, tones, and countenance by a loving regard for your happiness. Now shall it be alleged in disparagement of my love that it has evinced itself in no extraordinary deeds? in no surpassing emotion? If I have grieved you, how much feeling must I have before I make my confession and entreat your forgiveness? Is not that a suitable and adequate amount which, instantly upon my becoming conscious that I have so pained you, leads me frankly and honestly to own my fault and ask forgiveness? And is there one rule for our conduct towards man, and another towards Jesus? Can you see a fitness as towards man, and ignore such fitness as towards Jesus?

Do not weigh and measure your feelings, but do simply and ingenuously what seems to you right. Often say, "Dear Lord Jesus, I am very sinful, and very ignorant, but I mean to please Thee." You are just now realizing more vividly than usual how much "all the heart, soul, mind, and strength" means. And seeing how far short of that you have been willing to stop, you are tempted to condemn the love you have really borne your Lord, as naught. Now that is neither wise nor true. Moreover, it is ungrateful, for it refuses to recognize what He has actually done for you; and it would stop all praise. While praying last night, I thought of you. I felt so deeply the need of holiness, I realized anew your difficulty and mine, of stopping supplication in order to praise. But I reminded myself, as I now remind you, that He has done great things for us; and that we must and will praise Him.

If you are not careful, Satan will worry you into a fever of anxiety because there is so much to be done,—so much lost time to be made up. Many years ago, when the same insatiable desires were upon me that have laid hold on you, I wrote to Dr. Skinner for advice, and I must hand over to you his short prescription : "Mem. Restlessness is not holiness."

Quiet yourself in the Lord. Often recall to mind, that the most you have to do is to cast yourself on Him. He is really to do all. You are to hunger and thirst. You are doing so, and you are blessed in so doing. But you are to believe in His love, and to rest in His love. The yoke of Christ is easy, and His burden is light; and you have no right to make it oppressive, even to yourself. It is a great thing, a very great thing, to talk of Jesus as you are now sighing to do. I am only just beginning, as it seems to me, to talk of Him with any degree of facility. I have indeed all these years been talking of Him, and in some sort to Him, but so utterly short of what should have been! Such an absence of that heart-gushing tenderness, that fullness of appreciation which comes so promptly for a human friend! We will encourage one another, and we will not despise the day of small things, but be willing and thankful to increase from very small beginnings. The dear Lord will give us time enough to do what He has for us to do, and to become what He intends we shall become; therefore do not allow the Adversary, or your own impatience, to goad you into a fever. I have seen the evil of this. Worry comes of unbelief in Jesus and His unceasing care of us. Remember His assurance: "Thou wilt keep him in perfect peace whose mind is stayed on Thee; because he trusteth in Thee." As

I read on in your letter, I see that Satan is buffeting you. No wonder! he cannot bear to have you to take this new start. He would like to sift you as wheat. But hear His gracious assurance, who says, "I have prayed for thee, that thy faith fail not." His prayers are ever heard, and your faith will not fail.

You revive the conviction that the answer you desire can be given only to faith. Some one has said that a good book is not a work, but a growth. The same may be said, and truly, of faith. We have something to do with it, just as the farmer has much to do with preparing his field. But when he has done all he can do, God only can quicken the seed sown into life. The analogy here is, that, to the best of your ability, you separate yourself from all entanglements. You give your ear and your mind, as far as you can, to His Word; but only the Holy Ghost, the Comforter, can quicken it so that it shall come to you as the very word and love of Jesus, rooting itself in your heart, and growing vigorously. You know how it is when we love very dearly, and the love is fully reciprocated; our beloved one can do nothing, but what discovers love, let it look as it may to others. Only let it be thus between your soul and Jesus, and let Him send what He will, in answer to your prayers, it will come full charged and overflowing with His love to you.

A word about sorrow for the past. How much

sorrow is most suitable? Not so much as to carry you to the verge of despondency. Thither your last letter seemed to show you tending. Even a right exercise of mind may be turned to an evil, just by pressing it to an extreme. This is a common device of Satan. To look at your sinfulness long enough to despair of salvation by works, and to feel the need of Jesus, is well. But one clear sight of His forgiving love is more potent for good than a thousand sights of your sinfulness. I protest it is not true that you are nothing else but sin. Remember His own testimony: " So God made man in His own image;" also that Jesus ransomed you with His own life, and washed you in His blood; and for aught you can show, He may have chosen you to be a vessel of mercy to thousands.

Do not let any persuasion turn you from the use of endearing epithets applied to Jesus. Strange, passing strange, that any one can be so blinded as to believe that while the language of truest and tenderest affection may and ought to be lavished on parents, brothers and sisters, husband and wife, piety and propriety alike forbid that He who demands our whole heart, soul, mind, and strength, should be accosted with anything more tender and loving than the stilted and frigid language of courtly ceremony. My answer to all this is, Jesus is the chiefest among ten thousand, and altogether lovely; He is dear Jesus, sweet Jesus, precious Jesus, light of my eyes, joy of my heart, crown of my life.

Get thee behind me, Satan! Away with your miserable croakings; down to your own dark and loveless den!

"Lord of all being: throned afar,
Thy glory flames from sun and star;
Centre and soul of every sphere,
Yet to each loving heart how near!

"Sun of our life, Thy quickening ray
Sheds on our path the glow of day;
Star of our hope, Thy softened light
Cheers the long watches of the night.

"Our midnight is Thy smile withdrawn;
Our noontide is Thy gracious dawn;
Our rainbow arch Thy mercy's sign;
All save the clouds of sin are Thine!"

VI.

THANKSGIVING.

> "Good tidings every day,
> God's messengers ride fast.
>   We do not hear one half they say
>   There is such noise on the highway
> Where we must wait while they ride past.
>
> "Their banners blaze and shine
> With Jesus Christ's dear name
>   And story; how by God's design
>   He saves us in His love divine,
> And lifts us from our sin and shame."

THANKSGIVING DAY. — My heart is so full of joy and thanks this morning that it must have leave to overflow. If you could have looked in upon me half an hour ago, you might have thought me delirious, but I was never more rational. I was leaping for joy; joy for what our Lord has done for our nation, and for the indications of what He intends to do. Among my conscious occasions for overflowing thanks and praise to my dear, my precious, my honored, adored, revered Father, was His grace in permitting me to care for your spiritual weal; especially in permitting my attempts to show you how to see Jesus. I went to bed at midnight praying earnestly that He would crown you with every blessing, and awoke this morning full of happiness in the assurance that He will do so. I am sure of it. I turned to my favorite 145th Psalm, which seems ever to offer itself as the peculiar medium for the expression of a full heart, and read it, almost shouting with exultation. Then I turned to Colossians i. and renewed for you, and for myself, the prayer suggested in the ninth, tenth, and eleventh verses.

Indeed He is good, and "no good thing will He withhold from them who walk uprightly," — which means, those who in all their lives aim to please Him. What a precious assurance is that in Psalm cxviii. 6, "The Lord is on my side; I will not fear." Why should we not exclaim, "I love the Lord, because He hath heard my voice and my supplication: Because He hath inclined His ear unto me, therefore will I call upon Him as long as I live"?

You ask me not to be disappointed that you cannot say that the contest is over, and the victory won, and that a new light has dawned upon you.

So long as you hunger and thirst, none of these things move me. Your successful attempt to find in John xvii. our Lord's sweet utterances in your behalf, is an earnest of what He will do for you. When you have time to read the xiv., xv., and xvi. chapters in the same way, that is, hearing His voice in those passages as addressed to yourself, you will have a still more abundant revelation of His love and care for you.

Last summer I found a dear friend making a singular mistake; one that had never occurred to me as possible. She thought she had got to realize the person of Jesus, as one realizes General Washington, in Stuart's portrait of him. Of course you would not make that mistake, because you have been very differently trained. But it occurs to me to ask, what do you in fact expect? Possibly there may be something amiss in your expectation, which would explain your disappointment hitherto. The majority are hindered by indifference; but when, as in your case, there is no indifference, there is reason to conjecture the existence of some misapprehension, preventing that realization of Jesus which you say you have never had. There is a fundamental idea in "Butler's Analogy," which was very serviceable to me; that, namely, of its being the mind, and not the eye, that sees. If you are near-sighted, you use glasses. But the glasses do not see; and, the doctor adds, no more does the eye see; but the mind looks through the eye, and also, and in like manner, through the glasses. So again the mind moves matter. You push a ball on the floor with your hand, or, taking a cane you push it with the cane. In one case, as in the other, it is the mind that moves matter, "and it cannot be shown that matter was ever moved but by mind." It is thus we become accustomed to regard unseen powers as truly real and efficient, as things audible, visible, or tangible. Now, having made this truth your own, you go to your chamber to meet Jesus, your true living, loving Friend, whose form you have never seen, and do not care to see, because faith in God's testimony, loving trust in God Himself, makes Him so present and real that form and color could add nothing to the reality of His presence. You begin to treat Him as real. You address Him in a simple, frank, ingenuous manner. You speak in your natural voice and tone. Your reverence may subdue that tone; your love pervade it with tenderness; and a sense of the greatness of your privilege may make it tremulous with emotion. A better analogy for exercise of faith in this intercourse with Jesus could scarcely be had, than that which is supplied by the attempt to swim. If you have ever made that attempt, you have discovered that the one hindrance to swimming is distrust of the water; the difficulty of believing that that yielding element, so easily displaced, can be trusted to buoy up these heavy bodies of ours. The trained swimmer knows that it will. So he who is trained to lean and rest on Jesus knows that the invisible, impalpable arm and heart, is just as real and to be depended on, as any in the world; nay, far, far more; that for instant presence, availability, and strength, no other arm or heart can once be named in comparison with His. Now how shall you come to give this trust to your unseen Friend? — Heart-trust being, as you know, the truest sight of Jesus. I answer, it must be wrought in you. Faith is the gift of God to him who values and seeks it; and the place to seek it is in the Word of God, for therein He reveals Himself. Read there what He has said, and command your whole soul to receive both it and Him. Reading aloud with heart-utterance, will greatly aid you. I think I cannot too much insist that you are not to exaggerate the importance of emotion. With our training, you and I could not come to religion as Orient did; or as our beloved brother Paul came to his recognition of Jesus. Consider, it was all totally new to her. Her sensibility had not been frittered away, as mine, at all events, had been, by holding the truth in unrighteousness; by holding it as an abstraction, which I was bound to believe, but which, without honestly saying so, I was unwilling to obey. She never had the thousand and one presentations of the claims of Jesus, which I had practically ignored. It is no just argument against the reality of your piety or mine, that it is less emotional than Orient's or Paul's. The true test is to be found in the strength of our desire and purpose to be, to do, and to suffer all His will. And it does not follow that your heart is cold, because you are very quiet. Neither is James Brainerd Taylor's continuous ecstasy incumbent upon you. Be true to your occasions. That is all. If I had not seen a dear friend for years, ecstasy, on meeting, might be most appropriate. But if I see him every day, a genial smile or a cordial word would better become the occasion. I hope you are learning the worth of brief Scriptural lessons, lived on for days together. For more than a year I have found intense satisfaction in turning to Colossians i. 9, 10. At other times I have taken John xiv. 13, 14, as a basis of prayer. I have held up the book to Jesus with my finger on those verses, and asked Him, Dear Lord, didst Thou not say that? And wilt Thou fail to redeem Thy pledge? And then I have appealed to the Father, that I had Jesus's warrant. And then I have felt entirely sure that He could never fail me. Is He not dear Jesus? Precious Jesus? And won't you trust and love Him wholly?

VII.

GUIDANCE.

"I will guide thee with mine eye."— Ps. xxxii. 8.

"Wherever He may guide me,
No want shall turn me back;
My Shepherd is beside me,
And nothing can I lack."

I FIND in every letter you send me, unmistakable evidence that the Good Shepherd is leading you. Do not be over much troubled about "the weight which oppresses you." I have little doubt that its procuring cause is purely physical.

"Strange that a harp of thousand strings
Should keep in tune so long!"

Experience oft repeated has taught me whenever I find my Lord piling up obstacles, apparently insuperable, to the attainment of some desired object, He is but trying my faith. For Jesus is in all our obstacles revealing Himself to all who have eyes, heart-eyes to see Him. So, for a long time, I have become accustomed to find in accumulating obstacles only a love-token of His presence, and of His intention to give the thing desired. You say "you are a starving child, deterred from eating by the very abundance of what is offered." I have a message specially for you: "He that believeth shall not make haste." Fevered hurry, and fear of loss, come of distrust of God's kind intentions. A gentleman came into my office one day, just to say, "I think you will readily get Mr. M., if you call on him." My first and wonted impulse was to rush. But, remembering whose servant I was, and from whom the offered business really came, and that "he that believeth shall not make haste," I said to myself, Nay, but stop a little, and consider who will give what you will get; and that if it pleases Him to give, none can hinder; moreover, that it is fitting that I take it from Him, and not from my own dispatch, in which I am over apt to glory. And so I stayed my soul on Jesus, and then went quietly, trustfully, gratefully, and secured the business. You see the application of the principle, and you have frequent need to make it. Therefore, "be careful for nothing; but in everything by prayer and supplication, with thanksgiving, let your requests be made known unto God. And believe, — without looking for sign or token, — believe simply and alone on His promise, "Whatsoever ye shall ask in my name, that will I do," — and believing, give grateful thanks to your recognized Lord. This is seeing Jesus.

To the "pupil suddenly advanced from the alphabet to a difficult yet inviting lesson," I say, Do not be overwhelmed with the consciousness that "intermediate lessons are not mastered." No strange thing hath happened to you. It is no more your experience than mine. Remember that Jesus took you just as He found you, and will never taunt you with past remissnesses. I am unspeakably glad to hear you say, " I want to whisper 'Dear Jesus' in my heart, and feel His smile in return." Do not hesitate to do so. You shall have all that, beloved, and a great deal beside. See John i. 50; also 1 John i. 3; the last clause particularly.

You are doubtless familiar with Fénelon, but perhaps you have not met with the following extracts, which deserve to be treasured in letters of gold. They have been to me dear beyond expression.

"The purest prayer is nothing else than loving God. Oh how few there are who pray! For where are those who desire the true blessings? These blessings are exterior and interior crosses, humiliation, renunciation of one's own will, death to one's self, the reign of God on the ruins of self-love. Not to desire these things, is not to pray. To pray, it is necessary to desire them, seriously, really, constantly, and in reference to the whole detail of life; otherwise prayer is only an illusion; like a beautiful dream, in which the unhappy person rejoices, thinking that he possesses a felicity which is far from him. We never cease to pray so long as we do not cease to have the true love and the true desire in the heart. The love hidden in the depths of the soul prays without ceasing, even when the mind cannot be in actual attention." ["I sleep, but my heart waketh."] "God ceases not to regard in this soul the desire that Himself forms there, and which the soul itself does not always perceive. This desire in the disposition touches the heart of God; it is a secret voice that attracts without ceasing His mercies. This love entreats God to give us what we want, and to have less regard to our frailty than to the sincerity of our intentions. This love removes even our slight faults and purifies us like a consuming fire. It asks in us, and for us, that which is according to the will of God. For not knowing what we ought to ask for, we should often ask what would be hurtful to us. We should ask certain fervors, sensible satisfactions, and certain apparent excellences that would only serve to nourish in us the natural life and confidence in our own strength; whereas, on the other hand, this love, by leading us, by giving us up to all the operations of grace, and putting us in a state of entire surrender with regard to all that God shall will to do in us, disposes us for all the secret designs of God, then we wish all, and we wish nothing. What God shall wish to give us, is precisely what we shall have wished; for we wish all that He wills, and only what He wills. Thus this state contains all prayer.

It is an operation of the heart that embraces every desire. The Spirit asks in us what the Spirit Himself wills to give us. Then even when we are occupied without, and the necessary engagements of life produce in us an unavoidable distraction, we bear always within us a fire which is not extinguished, but which on the contrary nourishes a secret prayer, that is like a lamp burning without ceasing before the throne of God." Speaking of meditation on Divine truths he says: "These truths must penetrate us a long time, as the dye is gradually imbibed by the wool we would color. Then a single word, quite simply spoken, penetrates deeper than whole discourses. The same things that had been heard a hundred times coldly, and without any fruit, nourish the soul with a hidden manna, which has multiplied and varied tastes for days together. Indeed we must take care not to cease to nourish ourselves with certain truths by which we have been touched. Whilst there remains still any relish to us, while they still have anything to give us, it is a certain sign that we need to receive from them. They nourish us even without any distinct and precise instruction. They are something which effects more than all reasonings. We see a truth; we love it; we repose upon it; it strengthens the heart; it detaches us from ourselves; and here we should abide in peace as long as we can. In time our reflections and reasonings gradually diminish; affectionate sentiments, touching views and desires, increase. This is an evidence that we have been sufficiently instructed and convinced by the Spirit. The heart enjoys, is nourished, is warmed, is inflamed, a word only is necessary to occupy us a long time. At last, prayer goes on growing by views constantly more simple and fixed, so that we no longer have need of so great a multitude of objects and considerations. We are with God as with a friend. At first one has a thousand things to say to his friend, and a thousand things to ask him; but afterward this detail of conversation is exhausted without our being able to exhaust the pleasure of the intercourse. We have said all; but, without speaking, it is a pleasure to be together, to see each other, to feel that we are near, to repose in the enjoyment of a sweet and pure friendship. We are silent, but in this silence understand each other. We know that we agree in all, and that the two hearts are but one. The one is poured without ceasing into the other. It is thus that in prayer the intercourse with God becomes a simple and familiar union that is beyond all discourse. But it is necessary that God only should of himself effect this sort of prayer in us; and nothing would be more rash or more dangerous than to venture to introduce one's self into it."

I can only wish and pray, that this may prove to you as truly God given, as it certainly was to me, many years ago, when first placed in my hands. I have never met with anything more exquisitely beautiful, I do not mean the words, but the thing; nothing more admirably adapted to my conscious need; nothing out of the Bible which so met and satisfied the ideal suggested by the Bible. How beautifully it harmonizes with David's profession, "As the hart panteth after the water brooks, so panteth my soul after Thee, O, God." "Thou art my portion, O Lord." "How precious also are Thy thoughts unto me, O God! How great is the sum of them! If I should count them, they are more in number than the sand. When I am awake, I am still with Thee."

You say, "I used to think, if I could but be assured of an interest in Christ, I should be very happy." This thought is but one more testimony to what we know only too well, that at first we are sadly low and narrow in our desires. Personal safety is what we most think of. But if God has mercy upon us, and deals better with us than we deserve, He soon makes us ashamed of this, and we discover how ignoble it is to seek for nothing but future final salvation. I fully feel the truth of what you say of its being "a hard lesson — that of fear — to unlearn." But it is encouraging to remember that faith is not of yourself, but the gift of God; and He may give it you in a moment, and nothing is better suited to secure this gift than persistency in forgetting yourself, and in making the words and acts of the Lord Jesus your constant and loving study. Fill your mind with those divine declarations which warrant the resolution: "Come what may, I will not doubt His goodness, wisdom, honor, every generous sentiment." Why not so resolve? and firmly? There is much in making up one's mind to believe everything good of God. If you are not already familiar with the thought, make it a common thought, that if much requires to be done in you, the more it will honor Jesus to work out that which should be done. He is a Saviour to the uttermost for all who come unto God by Him. I do not remember if I have already quoted the passage, but I have derived immense support and consolation from our Saviour's declaration, John xvii. 10, "I am glorified in them." What an irresistible argument it is, thus put into our mouths! Father, remember that thy well beloved Son, my precious honored Lord, is glorified in my sanctification. John xvii. 17.

I have found it good to ask for holiness for holy purposes; that is, being watchful against selfish petitions, to ask to be made a vessel of mercy to many; and to this end, to be "filled with all the fullness of the blessed God."

I should like much were the thing possible — which indeed it is not — just to take the hand of a friend who wrote me yesterday, and putting it into yours, say, There, just talk it over with each other. What do you think she was puzzling about? She says: "You wrote me, in the Spring, that I must use endearing epithets in my communion with Jesus; and

I have; until now I am almost frightened by the temptation to love Him to the extent of forgetting reverence and awe. I have been searching the New Testament to find a warrant for such intimacy of affection and don't find it. He seems to me, on the contrary, to put the people off." Well, I did not wonder at her making that discovery; for it is there. When one came saying, "I will follow Thee whithersoever Thou goest," his service was declined. Doubtless he had not counted the cost. James and John were given to understand that that was their predicament. Peter was confident, but self-ignorant; and the Syrophenician woman, who was sound at the core, was given an opportunity to show to all the world that she looked beyond His words, into the heart of the speaker, and knew how to take her Lord. Even we ourselves, made in God's own image, cannot open ourselves to every one. Jesus would encourage only those who would forsake all for Him. A word about that struggle with unbelief which it cost you to conclude your letter with, "Your sister in Christ." I have often had occasion to say, I feel at this moment the Gospel would be no Gospel to me, if it did not come right down to my feet, to the low plane whereon I stand, meeting me where it finds me; my Lord saying to me, I invite you now. I offer to take you just as you are. Will you be mine? Will you put yourself unconditionally, unqualifiedly into my hands; submitting the transformation of yourself to my conduct? He puts the same question to you. If you assent, then it is your privilege at once to act the part of a believer. You have nothing to do with the matter of putting yourself on probation to see if you will hold out. That is the impulse of unbelief, against which, as an enlisted soldier of Jesus, you have declared war; war instant; war endless. Jesus wants your full heart's love; and He wants it now. And having Himself given you the undeniable warrant, in Mark xii. 30, there is not a shadow of a doubt of His offering you the utmost possible freedom of loving access to Him. John, the beloved, adds his plain testimony in his first Epistle (i. 3): "And truly our fellowship is with the Father and with his Son Jesus Christ." As I wrote to that dear sister, so let me say to you: There can, I think, be no loss of reverence and holy awe, in consequence of a greatly growing affectionate love providing only that there be reasonable pains taken to see Jesus as far as we can, in the whole range of his attributes. Remembering, that while He is "the man Christ Jesus," He is also "the brightness of the Father's glory, and the express image of His person;" that "all things were made by Him and for Him;" that "He knows every thought of man's heart;" that "the heavens are unclean in His sight;" and viewing Him as he appears in Psalms 45 to 50, and in the 139th, also in Job xxxviii., and on to the end of that book. But these are the references for another sort of spirit than yours. I do not think you are in danger of being presumptuous. I am much more apprehensive of your permitting awe to repress your love. You should listen to His assurance : " I am the rose of Sharon, and the lily of the valleys." And if you are beginning to find Him whom your soul loveth, you should hold Him fast, and not let Him go. He may, to try your faith, make as though he would go farther, and yet be well pleased to have you constrain Him to abide with you. Luke xxiv. 28, 29. My undoubting belief is, that you may have just as much love, and as much freedom to love Him, as you can appreciate. Try Him.

VIII.

TRIAL OF FAITH.

"Then shall we know, if we follow on to know the Lord."— HOSEA vi. 3

> "I cannot rest till in Thy blood
> I full redemption have;
> But Thou, through whom I come to God,
> Canst to the utmost save."

I FEEL perfectly sure that our Lord is, as you suggest, "trying your faith." It reminds me of my own experience in 1831. I was in earnest; I know I was in earnest; just as I am sure you now are. I tried in all ways to give myself to Jesus. I suspect I actually did give myself to Jesus before I realized the fact. In the retrospect it does not appear to me at all difficult to understand that there might be great good to be derived from a continuance in uncertainty. "Wait, I say, on the Lord." "It is good that a man should both hope and quietly wait for the salvation of the Lord." No, surely, we are ready to exclaim, you can't mean that it can be as good to wait, as instantly to receive what we seek!

When it did come, it came not as I anticipated, but fully, gloriously, and wholly of the Lord. Since then my experience has been that of your friend who "finds Christ so near that He can almost be touched." And yet that does not express it. You see why; because it falls back on the sense of touch, for an illustration. But He is nearer than that. John Foster speaking of friends says, "I will converse with my friends in solitude; then they seem to be within my soul; when I am with them they seem to be without it." I like this way of considering our relations to our beloved Jesus. My soul is a receiver; only exhaust or empty it, and the Holy Spirit will come in, as the air rushes into the exhausted receiver, when opportunity is offered. Our part is just to make room for Him. Only purely purge His temple, and you cannot keep Him out. You will perhaps be saying, Ah! that is what I cannot do; and must depend on Him to do it. Admit that; but one thing remains for you, namely, to will to do it. "He that shall come will come, and will not tarry." A Scriptural paradox, and not unintelligible; for he that comes in the best time, cannot be charged with delay. Doubtless you will have that sense of nearness you crave. And yet if my Heavenly Father finds something to be corrected by withholding the sense of His nearness, shall I prescribe to Him? Nay, Lord, but be it unto me even as Thou wilt. Now about your difficulty in attempting to read the fourteenth of John. I think the experience of the most spiritual persons I know shows this difficulty to be not uncommon. "One day you read, and find only words, words, words." Another day and you are saying, "Or ever I was aware, my soul made me like the chariots of Amminadib." As Fénelon testifies, "A line or a word will keep the soul a going a long time." President Edwards bids us "watch for the gales of the Spirit." Now this is not because God wishes to deal with us in an arbitrary way, but because it is immensely to our profit to become thoroughly aware of our utter dependence upon Him. You will often find when you cannot read a chapter to advantage, you can read a single verse. I make a point of fastening upon a verse, or even a word that fixes my attention. Thus I have found the "Daily Food" often very useful because of its shutting me up to one verse or two. Persist in making your verse reading an actual conference with Jesus. Thus when you read: "He that hath my commandments and keepeth them, he it is that loveth me," say to Him, "Dear Jesus, I have Thy commandments; I love them; I try to keep them; very imperfectly do I succeed, dear Lord, that I must own. But it is my grief; I confess to Thee frankly, and with no attempt at palliation. And Thou hast said that if we confess our sins, Thou art faithful and just to forgive us our sins and to cleanse us from all unrighteousness." You might go on, if you chose, to enlarge upon your unworthiness of favor, and contrast with this the desert of God's dear Son. But better than this, would it not be, if dropping all consideration of yourself you could give undivided thought to the attractive characteristics of your Lord. You will find scores and hundreds of passages in the Bible particularly suited to aid you in doing this. Take for example the nineteenth Psalm. "The heavens declare the glory of God, and the firmament showeth His handiwork." Familiar as this truth is to you, its power to interest is by no means exhausted. Every successive sunset and sunrise brings new pleasure to you. You cannot forget the assurance in the first chapter of Colossians that all things were made by Him, your own loving Lord, by Him, and for Him. And the speech concerning Him and His works, which day utters unto day, is intelligible and sweet to you. Every item of knowledge of Him and of His works may surely bind you more closely to Him; may quicken and intensify your admiration and love. And when you pass from the works of material creation to those of mind and heart, will not your appreciation rise to a higher and warmer type? With David you will be enforced to exclaim: "The law of the Lord is perfect, converting the soul: the testimony of the Lord is sure, making wise the simple. The statutes of the Lord are right, rejoicing the heart: the commandment of the Lord is pure, enlightening the eyes. The fear of the Lord is clean, enduring forever: the judgments of the Lord are true and righteous altogether." You will naturally

— I was going to say inevitably — fasten upon the thousand and one instances supplied by the incidents of your own family and personal history, as illustrating these attributes of your Lord: "More to be desired than gold, yea, than much fine gold: sweeter also than honey and the honey-comb." Is not this seeing Jesus? And is it not a precious and affecting sight? Is it not strange that we spend so much time and strength deploring our own unworthiness, our backwardness especially to love our Lord, when the very time and strength thus consumed in regrets, were it given to the study of His Word, to the study of Himself as disclosed in His Word, would suffice to raise our love to a great height?

How would it be possible, for example, to read frequently, to commit to memory and to heart, as we easily might, the fourteenth and fifteenth chapters of John, and not be convinced beyond all possibility of doubt, that Jesus' love to us is beyond all comparison, for sweetness, for tenderness, for endurance, and for painstaking. True, we may neutralize all this evidence, precisely as we may neutralize the evidence of human friendship, by trampling upon, or by neglecting it. Evidently the antidote to distrustful thoughts and anxious solicitudes is to be found in the diligent study of our God, in all His providences, in His works, and above all in His word. You say, "The day passes on; I do not think happy loving thoughts of Jesus, perhaps think little about Him in any way." To this I reply, you have in former letters made reference to physical exhaustion and depression. No doubt this has much to do with the religious experiences you regret. Indeed, I question, if these should be called religious experiences. You may, however, make them such in quoting His own words: " Shall there be evil in the city and the Lord hath not done it ? " and in submitting your soul, with, Not my will, dear Lord, but Thine be done, I do not think that " you must conclude something is amiss in your desires, or in your consecration, because you cannot immediately say, I love the Lord," etc. A deep work of grace in your heart may require a measure of suspense. If you attained at once, on your first asking, what would satisfy your longing, you might relax your endeavors and make little further progress. It certainly is not " wrong for you to look for and to covet some degree of conscious love ; " and yet I would guard against anxious looking even for that. Loving trust in Jesus and His promises, is the one thing needful, and the earnest study of Jesus, to know Him more fully, to get better hold of some trait already known, or a clear apprehension of some trait not hitherto considered. Dismiss for the time, as far as you can, what Christians tell you of their conscious nearness, and try to see Jesus with your own eyes as He reveals Himself, for example, in the chapters in John to which I have just referred, or in any others which attract you. Expect the Comforter to fulfill to you the promises Jesus makes on His behalf, namely, that He shall guide you into all truth. When you pray to Him, do not make your praying to Him very different from simple talking with Him. Accept the fact, on Jesus' statement, that you have the Comforter with you always; "that He may abide with you forever." It seems to me that you may cling to the fact, even when you cannot secure the consciousness you crave. Do not say, or think, that your prayers can avail nothing in my behalf. This saying is one more revelation of the subtle mischief of unbelief; I should rather say of the evil arising from long indulged erroneous views of your actual relations to God. You speak as if your prevailing in prayer depended upon what you are; whereas it depends upon what Jesus has done, and is doing: "He ever liveth to make intercession." As for ourselves, "Ye are my witnesses, saith the Lord." And Jesus adds: "Whatsoever ye shall ask in my name, that will I do." You can surely plead for me and mine in Jesus' name; in His interest, for the furtherance of His wishes. And in thus pleading you will lay me under the highest obligations.

IX.

GOD'S MINUTE CARE.

> " As individual stars are we
> Set out in God's infinity,
>   With cyclic ways about His throne
> What if the mystic, spheric course
> Drawn by His silent, unseen force,
>   Swerve out beyond thy ken in the unknown ? "

YOU cannot doubt that " He who spared not His only begotten Son, but freely gave Him for you, will with Him also freely give you all things." But, you tell me, you think your belief of this great undeniable truth, like your belief in the law of gravitation, by reason of its very breadth and universal application, almost wholly fails to control you. Evidence of infinitely less love touches you deeply, when it comes in the looks and tones of those who are about you.

Well, communion with God, walking with God, loving God with all the heart, soul, mind, and strength, does not appear to be natural to most of us, does it? And the confident assertions of some, that human nature is not a fallen nature at all, but a very good nature, lacking nothing but cultivation and development, will not bring conviction to your mind or mine; no, not to any one who is earnestly set on pleasing God. Such an one is much more likely to point to the exclamations of St. Paul, as expressing what he finds to be painfully true: "How to perform that which is good, I find not. For the good that I would, I do not, but the evil which I would not, that I do." But surely it is no small consolation to find that in sturdy resistance to these wayward propensities, is the path of virtue. In persistent endeavors to conform our lives to the will of God, and to the beautiful example of the Lord Jesus, we are cultivating that which ennobles and purifies us. We find also the unmistakable evidence of God's nearness, of His intimate acquaintance with all our needs, of His ceaseless, minute, and tender care for us. When in the retrospect we clearly see that He has "led the blind by a way they knew not," we are moved by the love that would not be alienated even by our unbelief; but patiently followed us with renewed, multiplied, and patient manifestations of more than maternal love. "Fear not," He says, "not a sparrow falls to the ground without your Father; ye are of more value than many sparrows; the hairs of your head are all numbered." Be assured you are not lost in the crowd of His creatures. His heart is set on drawing you into that close fellowship with Himself which must of necessity be more to you than all beside. Naturally, it seems to you, that you alone desire such fellowship. You are ready to exclaim,

Oh that I could indulge the hope that He would care for this as I do! So as young children, how often we sighed out, Oh, if my father or mother would only give me this or that, it would make me so happy! Only when we in our turn have become parents, do we begin to realize how greatly a parent's loving carefulness exceeds all possibility of the child's conjecture. When I look back to the little and larger incidents of my youth, the incidents which made the warp and the woof of my young life, long before my conversion, before I had begun to consider God's interest and purpose in my life, those incidents assume an interest and an importance which cannot be exaggerated. They are just so many unmistakable tokens of His definite, far-seeing, thoughtful, loving care. "Behold what manner of love the Father hath bestowed upon us, that we should be called the sons of God! Beloved, now are we the sons of God." Behold His purpose, resolved upon and adopted long before we ever entertained the thought, now carried into effect! To all this He subjoins, and upon this He rests His moving appeal: "Let not your hearts be troubled, ye believe in God, believe also in me." And He who makes this appeal is the same of whom it is written: "By Him were all things created, that are in heaven, and that are in earth, visible and invisible, whether thrones, dominions, principalities, or powers; all things were created by Him, and for Him." Why you should seem to yourself to be separated from this loving Friend, it is not easy, perhaps not possible, to affirm. It surely is not unreasonable to conjecture, that it is for the nurture of that faith which clings all the closer to the unseen. It has been well said by one of old time: "He that watches for providences"—meaning unmistakable tokens of God's constant, minute, personal care—"shall have providences." The self-styled philosophers, who can find no analogies in God's natural works to warrant such expectation, do but convict themselves of being very heedless observers of those works.

This morning I received a letter from the dear friend who was fearful of loving Jesus too familiarly, in which she says: "Did you never look out upon a landscape, or upon some beautiful painting, and gaze until your whole soul was lost in it—you were not conscious of individual existence? I have had such moments in thinking of Jesus. No sense of sin; no realization of imperfection; lost to everything but His presence. Well, the night I got your letter, I prayed God, with tears of penitence, never to let me have them again." And she writes thus because I, in my feeble and inadequate endeavors to indicate to her the true medium, must have miserably failed. Else how could the dear child imagine that I could have anything but joy in her being thus absorbed in Jesus? The Lord help me to avoid discouraging His lambs.

X.

LOOKING TO JESUS.

"At evening time it shall be light." — ZECH. xiv. 7.

"Up to the hills I lift mine eyes,
There all my hope is laid;
The Lord who built the earth and skies, —
From Him will come mine aid."

YOU need have no "fear that my heart will grow heavy at the sight of your familiar hand," for I receive each familiar letter as a fresh token of the love of Him who gave Himself for us. You will not think me unfeeling if I tell you, that I have been both sorry and glad that "you have been in deeper darkness ever since reading my previous letter," because I recognize your Guide through the darkness. This is His way. He goes before you. He stands, as upon the lake He stood before Peter, and bids you come to Him upon the waves. "Fear not, little one, it is your Father's good pleasure to give you the kingdom." Most gladly would I have had that hour's talk with you which you craved. Say to Jesus just what you would have said to me. He is perhaps plunging you into "the night of faith." It was in Thomas à Kempis, if I remember rightly, that I found that expression. Jesus taught me its meaning, and to regard the experience as being of exceeding worth. Do you not discern a foreshadowing of it in Genesis xv. 12? Then, as now, it was a prelude to great blessings to come. Stay your soul upon Psalm cxii. 4. "Unto the upright there ariseth light in the darkness." So have I found it, and so will you. When do we best realize the beauty of the heavens? Is it not when the stillness and the darkness of night is upon us? In the seeming darkness which you now bewail, the Star of Bethlehem is just about to shine upon you.

Sometimes in the midst of an attempt to comfort one of His beloved ones, I am startled by a sudden impression of the absurdity of any attempt of mine to show His love, whose love throws all my showings into utter obscurity. It is not merely true that "you will one day see the love of Jesus," but that you will soon see it. It is because you have not heretofore seen clearly your warrant to expect what you now desire, that you have not sooner won soul-satisfying views of the loveliness of Jesus. Do not put those views far away in the future, as though you must needs be long in coming up to them. Let me beg you again to cherish great expectations. Our blessed Lord is only trying you, to see if you really care for the great boon you are asking. Not that He needs the evidence, but you need it; and principalities and powers in heavenly places need it, and are waiting to see Him redeem His promise: "Then shall ye know, if ye follow on to know the Lord." Be firmly resolved that when He has tried you, He shall not find you wanting in trust. But if you are asking, Ah, how can I be sure? then take up His own divinely furnished words, "I can do all things through Christ who strengtheneth me." Not only do not go back of your consciousness, but do not go back to past experiences. Let us suppose the worst,— that you have never really made a total gift of yourself to Jesus. We may begin at this point. Blessed Saviour! He calls thee now. "Come, for all things are now ready." Sit right down to His feast. Never lose a moment in bemoaning yourself over the past. His arms are wide extended to you. Will you come? The prolonging of your painful experience is by no means a denial of your request. Every heart-breaking desire of yours, "Oh that I knew where I might find Him!" is a nearer approach to that emptying of your heart for Him, which absolutely insures your receiving your desire, and hastens the hour. Then do not scruple to renew and to augment your desires to see and embrace Jesus. Be assured I shall give Him no rest until He enables you to write me, "I have found Him." "I have found Him whom my soul loveth."

What you want is, "Christ in you." That is just what He desires for you. Is this mystical? Certainly its meaning is hidden from the natural man.

God says that. But Jesus Himself adds, "To you it is given." To know God and Jesus Christ is eternal life. He prays for you, and declares that He is glorified in His disciples, that is in you. Paul prayed for the Colossians, "that they might be filled with the knowledge of His will." This is to be freely received, as a most free gift. You cannot fill yourself with such knowledge and such love, but you can be filled. There are persons disposed to be indolent and self-excusing, on whom it were needless or unwise to press this, seeing they are predisposed to pervert it. I have no fear in saying it to you, because you are earnestly craving what our Lord desires to give you. Be it that He is sovereign and influenced in His gifts and revelation of Himself by some considerations not shown to us; yet to you He has given most significant intimations of His wish to be seen and known by you. Your hunger and thirst for this, is a sure earnest of it.

There is a state of mind and heart which may be characterized as self-emptied. Get it, if you can. Fasting helps to it. If total fasting disables you, as I think it would be likely to do, eat a cracker, or three, if you choose. An invalid should not attempt that which is suited only to the needs of those who are in sturdy health. To be emptied of self is most desirable. This does not imply any high wrought emotion. It implies only a clear perception of the lesson, "What hast thou that thou didst not receive?" and the earnest desire to remember this lesson. See Psalm cxxxi.: "Surely I have behaved and quieted myself as a child that is weaned of his mother. My soul is even as a weaned child." Get to this, and Jesus will grow up in you. Seeing is not so much the right word as some other. Trust Jesus wholly, and keep trusting Him. Act steadily and persistently on the assumption that He is entirely trustworthy. The inevitable consequence will follow in God's best time, and that will not be long in coming. I have complete sympathy in your having no wish to repeat past experiences. No doubt some lessons are best learned through many repetitions, but many experiences we may reasonably expect to leave behind us. Every year of my life is better than its predecessors. I am ever expecting the greater things divinely promised, and my expectations are as constantly exceeded.

In praying for you to-night I am again led to wonder if you are not delaying your peace in believing in Jesus, through the expectation of some sensuous impression of Him. The thing to be coveted is simply a controlling confidence in Him as a real, present friend. I would illustrate thus: A slight degree of confidence in a friend you had never seen, might obviously be increased by the presentation of facts adapted to establish the character of that friend. Such evidence of character would not necessarily bring any form before you.

It might remind you of some one you have known possessing like characteristics; and as the material form, like the name, stands for and represents the individual person, either the one or the other might be brought to your mind's eye by the recital of his own or like characteristics. This, I say, might come incidentally. But the thing of vital importance, in respect to your Lord, is not this, but an unwavering confidence in His friendship for you; in His nearness, His accessibility, and His availability for any and every need. This confidence evidently comes not from any excitation of the imagination, from any vision of form or features, but from the diligent study, and simple and hearty belief in His words, and in Himself as that self is made out from the study of His words and of His life. When you read that Jesus had compassion on the multitudes who had followed Him into the wilderness; that He would not send them away hungry, knowing that divers of them had come from far, you realize Him as being pitiful and compassionate; and so count with confidence on His pity for yourself in your own hour of need. The story of blind Bartimeus fosters this confidence; so does that of the man at the pool of Bethesda; Jesus' visit to Zaccheus; His kindness to the woman which was a sinner; to the man possessed with devils; and to a multitude beside. The conviction produced and fostered by the indwelling Comforter, Jesus in like manner cares for me, and for all my needs, penetrates your heart; and you reason of your own personal relations to Him thus:—

"I have need of His healing mercies for my soul. I will come to Him. He will have mercy on me as readily as on any of them." Thūs your faith lays hold of Him. Your faith turns into word and act, and becomes a practical thing. Jesus says, "Come!" you come. He says, "Cast your care on me!" you cast it on Him. He says, "Be careful for nothing!" you cast away all care, and begin with thanksgiving to let your requests be known unto Him.

XI.

TRIALS.

"Whom the Lord loveth, He chasteneth."— Heb. xii. 6.

"Wish not, dear friends, my pain away —
   Wish me a wise and thankful heart,
With God in all my griefs to stay,
   Nor from His loved correction start."

"I welcome all Thy sovereign will,
   For all that will is love;
And when I know not what Thou dost,
   I wait the light above."

I KNOW well what "a case of conscience" is. I shall never forget the two weeks of suspense in which our Lord held me, upon the question of trying for "the ministry." I remember the sheet of paper, on one page of which I set down the arguments for; and on the other, the arguments against it. Full well do I remember the mental wear and tear, and, finally, the inexorable necessity of coming to a decision, because, not to decide was to confess one's self an imbecile. Nor did the trial of faith end there. For three years thereafter I was required to take one step at a time, always with the conviction, I have received only permission to try. Now the natural man would claim this as a failure on God's part to redeem his pledges of direction. You and I know better. The discipline of mind and heart is, after all, what we most need; and that we get; and not only that, but we are infallibly directed. How often we are told by hasty and heedless speakers: "The way of duty is easily found when you have the disposition to walk in it." To such I reply, I have not so learned Christ. He has nowhere promised me that. He has indeed assured me of infallible guidance, but not a word has He said of the way being easily found. On the contrary, He has made me know that sometimes it is found only with great painstaking, and heart-searchings. He has taught me that He "leads the blind by a way they know not." He has often led me by a thread so fine that I could not see it. From your prolonged delay of decision, I have no doubt He is thus leading you. What an opportunity this gives for simple faith. The very grace we most wish to cultivate. Sometimes we find persons who profess to have sought God's guidance, giving up the decision they reached, — that is, giving up God's hand in it, — because they found "hills of difficulty," instead of a garden and bower of ease. This is surely to be faithless. I have found the path in which the Lord led me, hills of difficulty and all, to be the right way. Ps. cvii. 7. In 1845 I asked the Lord, "Shall I go to Europe, on business, or not? I am in debt, and would fain avoid a deeper immersion in that mire. Guide me, dear

Lord, to that result which will most glorify Thee." He influenced me to go. My business plunged me twice as deep in debt; involving much painfulness beside. But He bade me have faith in God; and so I did; I never doubted Him or His guidance; and He vindicated Himself and His guidance. I pray Him to lead you by a silken thread, ever so fine, but strong enough to hold you, provided you do not pull from, but with Him. "I will guide thee with mine eye," He says. And so He will; and you will be led in "the right way," because you desire first of all to honor Him.

A word about Jesus' knowing beforehand all that you could say to Him. Does not your husband know all your love for him? And yet is he so satisfied with that knowledge as to be indifferent to renewed expressions of trust and confidence? Moreover, is it not pleasant to go again and again to him with an unsettled question? Is it any less so, to go to Jesus with it? And does Jesus value your loving and trustful confidence less than your husband does? Disabuse yourself of this idea, that "intercourse with Jesus is so unlike that with visible friends." It does not oppress me at all, that Jesus knows it all beforehand. On the contrary, I delight in remembering that very fact. Obedience is better than all the philosophy in the world. He bids me come and tell Him; "Pray without ceasing;" "In everything by prayer and supplication, with thanksgiving, let your requests be made known unto God."

So I take everything to Him. My forenoon's experience qualifies me to say with emphasis, there is no progress without suffering. Among the letters of my dear boy, now in heaven, I find one written two or three years ago, in which he says: "I have been reading Flavel; and he makes me feel very uncomfortably. He teaches that we must fear all the time, and be forever keeping our own hearts. Now I cannot refute what he says, but I am sure that is very far from what I have been doing." This dear boy had his trials, as you have yours. And I am sure I have not got beyond this kind of trial. Many a day I am almost on the very verge of asking the Lord to let me lie down and die. Life's work is irksome. I have not physical force enough to like this roughing it in competition with men whose faculties are trained to the one business of accumulating money. But presently I think, I am where my Lord wishes me to be. Would I be willing to take my education and all its appliances out of His hands? No, never, never, never! Behold Thy servant, Lord; be it unto me even as thou wilt, "all the days of my appointed time will I wait, till my change come." Dear James's instinct was superior to something in Flavel's teaching which his experience did not enable him to refute. He came upon one of the Scripture paradoxes. "Pray without ceasing," and "Watch unto prayer," "Be careful for nothing;" "Trust in the Lord at all times;" and "Rest in the Lord." The watchfulness that should be taught, that of one friend, jealous about whatever would injure the interest or happiness of another friend, is entirely compatible with rest, trust, and joy. If Flavel taught that we must fear all the time, he was bound to define the fear and show it to be the fear of reverence only. It must comport with rest and trust and praise and peace. The only "keeping the heart all the time," divinely inculcated, must comport with and include, "keeping yourselves in the love of God, building yourselves up on your most holy faith, and praying in the Holy Ghost." I am inclined to think that unconsciously to yourself, you have been almost insisting that God should let you see your progress. But it is written: "The kingdom of God cometh not with observation." You are quite right in being inflexibly resolved on progress; but you may err in not being content to do and be what He commands, and infer the progress from His promise, while nothing meets your eye. Read Heb. xi. 13. May it not be that this has been your trouble for months past? And yet this cannot be all; "For flowers need night's cool darkness, the moonlight and the dew;" and in the natural world are many analogies for what we find in the spiritual life. I speak of the experiences of those who greatly desire "to walk worthy of the Lord unto all pleasing." Take my own case: the Lord permits, and appoints me to plod on in a business not very congenial, and so monopolizing of time and mental strength, that but little is left for what we are apt to deem higher avocations. Now I might ask, why, since it has pleased Him to give me an earnest desire to be a son of consolation, and a helper of His lambs and sheep, does He not give me respite from these absorbing cares, and leisure to do the good I would? But I have long since ceased asking or thinking that, because He makes me comprehend, in order to be of service to the suffering ones, I must acquire fellowship with them through companionship with them in their trials. Perhaps you may find in this necessity, the reason for your not immediately attaining the liberty you are longing for. Suppose the Lord should say to you: My dear child, all that you crave, I will most assuredly bestow. I commend you for the craving. I bid you "covet earnestly the best gifts;" but suppose that I see it best, in granting your desire, to place you in the company of sufferers, who, like Cowper, have ministered immeasurably to the comfort and spiritual wealth of others, while yet for themselves wholly unable to taste the consolation. It must have been at the sore cost of his own desolation, that Cowper learned to sing, "There is a fountain filled with blood." In resigning yourself wholly to the will of our Lord, cost what it may, you are as truly a martyr as though you were burnt at the stake. You cannot offer your service and yourself to Him and fail to be instantly accepted. To every one thoroughly in earnest it must appear, that no one's progress was ever so slow as his own. But every earnest endeavor to do God's will, is progress.

Congratulate me that our Father has given me again my Monday evening Bible Class. I have reason to have great satisfaction in this class; for the lady who opens her parlor and invites the class is a devout Baptist. Half or three quarters of the class, I presume, are Baptists. Two or more at the beginning of last winter were strong Unitarians. Before the winter was over, "the disciple whom Jesus loved," had convinced them of the essential deity of His Master. I delight in classes in which all denominational distinctions are ignored. In my Sunday morning class I have often had four and sometimes five denominations. The same is true of my Tuesday afternoon class. I never stay away from either class for storm of any kind or magnitude; so don't withhold your prayers for the classes on account of weather. In the Saturday evening class of young men, I have generally from twenty-five to thirty-five.

Your saying that "the reading of President Edwards's resolutions amazed you; that it looked burdensome, this making a business of religion," reminded me of my dear James's saying much the same once. Neither do I think it incumbent on you to adopt the whole 'Seventy Resolutions;' but it is worth much to have even read them. And when I go home to heaven I shall want to take an early opportunity to tell him how much they have contributed to guide and strengthen me. Have you thought of these as deriving their force from some Divine precept readily found in the Bible? Is there a stronger or more exacting thing among them all than this: "Thou shalt love the Lord thy God with all thy heart, soul, mind, and strength?"

Are you familiar with "John Foster's Essays on Decision of Character?" After the Bible I do not know of any book that has done me so much good. If you "have not yet come into any liberty," just look up to Jesus now, and ask Him: Dear Lord, where is that liberty you promise? How shall I come by it? Are you not as willing to give it to me as to the Galatians? And when, dear Lord? Why not now?

Why not, indeed? You have His answer in Romans viii. 1: "There is therefore now no condemnation to them who are in Christ Jesus." I suspect, my dear friend, that your faith halts upon the forgiveness of sins. Surely it ought not. You know 1 John i. 7, and also verse 9. You know that the Son of Man has been lifted up as the brazen serpent was. If you have not mastered that, you ought. Indeed, there is no substitute for just beginning at the beginning. When your Arithmetic or Algebraic problem does not come to a full solution, you go patiently back to the very beginning. Apparently you have assumed something of which you have never been fully convinced. What is that something? You should know. Search and find it. Do not fear to name it, if you suspect it. It is undoubtedly true that you have done too much of the "keeping yourself up to the mark." You say, "The Comforter has taught you many things the past two months; but you do not see that you have learned the one lesson, — Jesus." Let me interpret for you. You mean to say, that your sensibility toward Jesus has not in that time become what you desire. I can't say I am surprised at that. I suspect your soul has been more exercised by attempts to get near Jesus, than your understanding has been enlightened by an improved knowledge of some one or more of His adorable characteristics. Your solicitude to make progress has been so deep and constant that you could not forget yourself and the question of progress; but could you have wholly forgotten your own interest in the matter, and have been wrapt in the study, for example, of "the meekness and gentleness of Christ," might not your love have been inflamed to that degree that it would have devoured all your doubts? Introspection is doubtless sometimes indispensable; but too much of it is a bar to all progress in the knowledge and love of our Lord Jesus Christ. I do not remember whether we have talked of the necessity of communicating to others, as fast as we ourselves receive. I believe there is no substitute for this, and no dispensing with it. It is the law of the road on which we have resolved to travel. From what you have said, I have received the impression that you have in this way endeavored to do good and communicate, as you conceived that you had opportunity; but it is more than probable that you have often supposed yourself incompetent to speak for Jesus, because your knowledge of Him has been so unsatisfactory to yourself. You may have erred in this. You might and should tell what you know; and, moreover, you should be adventurous in your endeavors to be useful. You have the right to put forth exertions, counting upon Jesus to give you words and wisdom. For family prayers I have just opened at the ninth of Luke, and find Jesus telling the disciples, "Take nothing for your journey, neither staves, nor scrip, neither bread, neither money;" and it seemed to me most apropos. Here are many holding back from service on the ground that they are not furnished for their work. Now to connect with this the "liberty" you were sighing for; let me ask, How are you to come into the highest exercise of liberty, except in casting off all other dependence, and launching out fearlessly upon the broad sea of Christian effort, in simple dependence upon Jesus?

XII.

REVIVED FAITH.

"O beauteous things of earth!
  I cannot feel your worth
    To-day.
O kind and constant friend!
  Our spirits cannot blend
    To-day.

"O Lord of truth and grace!
  I cannot see Thy face
    To-day.
A shadow on my heart
  Keeps me from all apart
    To-day.

"Yet something in me knows
  How fair creation glows
    To-day.
And something makes me sure
  That love is not less pure
    To-day.
And that the Eternal Good
  Minds nothing of my mood
    To-day.

"For when the sun grows dark,
  A sacred, secret spark
    Shoots rays.
Fed from a hidden bowl,
  A lamp burns in my soul
    All days."

I AM more and more persuaded every hour, that we need nothing, absolutely nothing, but simple, affectionate, trustful faith in our blessed, sweet, noble, honored Redeemer. I went to church-meeting last evening feeling that perfect silence would best become my circumstances. But when brother W. read from Matt. xvi. 24: "If any man will come after me, let him deny himself, and take up his cross, and follow me," such a sense of the sweet privilege of following Jesus came over me, that I could not sit still; I must needs get up and tell them how sweet it was to follow always and only Jesus, and how rich the reward. How He was as good as His word, when He assured us that if any man would seek first the kingdom of God and His righteousness, all things should be added to him; he should have a hundred fold now in this time, and in the world to come, life everlasting.

Your mention of New Haven, warms my heart. I shall never forget how, in the winter vacation, Professor Goodrich had a few of us who remained in College, up in a recitation-room in the old Lyceum, and read to us the eightieth Psalm: "Give ear, O Shepherd of Israel." A revival began, it seemed to me, in the very reading of that Psalm, and in the prayers that followed. It was in January, 1835. Excuse this poor note. I felt as if I had finished my work, when I came to my office for a few moments to get my letters, and said to myself, what better, what more congenial thing can I do before I go home and bury my dead, than sit down in this corner and write a few words to my dear sister in Christ? Hope thou in God, for thou shalt yet praise Him with an overflowing and abounding heart of praise, for that He is the health of thy countenance and thy God. In this very trial of your faith, this decision reached in the dark, I find Him having respect unto your prayer, "Lord, increase my faith." "Lord show Thyself to me." He is doing it, and He will. He is drawing thee to Himself by cords of love, and you shall be joined to Him in closest affinity. Only believe, and trust, and love.

Thank you for your kind confidence. I feel that it becomes me to pray more earnestly, every day, to our Heavenly Father, that I may be worthy to deserve it. I am exceedingly interested in the way in which you are being led. Depend upon it, it means much. There is no waste of material in the Divine economy. It is therefore not for nothing that you have been thus held in suspense. I cannot have a doubt that great and good results are coming out of this, and you are being disciplined rightly to accept the results, and give God all the glory. The same mail which brought me your letter, brought also a kind letter of sympathy from Professor S., and another from one of my former Bible class pupils, now a matron and mother of quite a family in P. I must tell you a little about her. A. came into my Bible class one Sunday morning, out of a Unitarian family, her heart burdened and thirsting for some knowledge of Christ and His service. It was my blessed privilege to aid her in her search. At the first she was timid and distrustful of her prospects for spiritual life; fearful of not holding out; but all the while most diligently endeavoring to grow in grace. From a timid and uninstructed inquirer, she has gone steadily on, becoming after a year or two, a strong and noble Christian, full of faith and good works. Almost every member of her father's family followed her lead, and united with evangelical churches. Her mother once said to me, " I suppose you thought me very cross when you came to the house to see A. I did not comprehend the matter then. I do now, and I want you to convert my J." The Lord converted him, through the influence of a good Christian brother who was in the warehouse with him, and he is a clergyman now. But dear A. is one of the strongest and most useful Christians I know; and I well remember when she was far less advanced than you now are. That is the point of my story for you. Only hold on, and you will certainly grow stronger and stronger, for the mouth of the Lord hath spoken it. The time is steadily approaching when I shall say to some other seeker: There is E. once she was timid and doubtful about many things—most of all about herself, and her prospects spiritually — and now, see what God hath wrought! You will have become strong as an angel of God. For, "this is the will of God, even your sanctification." He will accomplish it; and you will have no false modesty or hesitancy in acknowledging the work of God.

You desire some book that shall take you up from the beginning. I could not name any one book that would do this. Do you own "Mason on Self-Knowledge?" I got valuable hints from that. I have no doubt that I got valuable hints from the "Westminster Catechism." I know I got great good from the "Memoir," and from the "Select Thoughts" of Dr. Payson; and so may any one who will use good sense, and discriminate between the doings of the Lord, and the doings of indigestion; between reasonable use of flesh and blood, and brains, and unreasonable use thereof, — H. W. B. to the contrary notwithstanding. I got good from "James Brainerd Taylor," and so may you, if you will guard against the error of endeavoring to make continuous the ecstasy of religious emotion. I do not believe, however, there is any way in which you will grow so fast, as in reading the Book of books; not by chapters, but by verses, and parts of verses which the Spirit makes fresh and interesting to you. I think I told you how much I have been living for a year past on Colossians i. 9, 10, turning these verses into a prayer for myself. It was the Comforter who one morning, in answer to prayer to Him for a blessing on my reading, made these verses spring up in my soul like living waters from a deep spring. The Comforter will do as much for you, if asked; may do it any hour, and is likely to do it, if you earnestly ask Him. Ask, and ask, and ask, again: "That He will fill you with the knowledge of His will, in all wisdom, and spiritual understanding; that you may walk worthy of the Lord unto all pleasing; being fruitful in every good work, and increasing in the knowledge of God." Could there be a more comprehensive expression of your heart's desire than this? And when you ask, believe. Is there any difficulty in this? Could you not ask me for anything in your heart, and believe too? Treat Jesus as well. Will you not? Live on the verses that win you. It is safe. Are you improving in praise? Certainly the translation of my heart's jewels has opened the fountains of praise anew, and sunk the well deeper. I read, and shout (privately) the 103d and the 145th Psalms. If you can bring your mind to it, I think it will be of infinite benefit to you to take up the leading points of Christian faith, which it may never have occurred to you to doubt, and turn up the Scripture passages which teach them; settling each one upon your own personal investigation, taking nothing for granted, as is, alas! too common. In this way, you will come to feel the solid rock under you. The deity of Christ, the perfect satisfaction made by His atoning sacrifice, and the forgiveness of sins to all who confess and believe; the indwelling of the Comforter, the certain efficacy of prayer, the acceptability of praise; the reality and sphere of faith; the absolute certainty of your salvation — as a believer; the certainty and greatness of God's love, the extent and certainty of His Providence. Rom. viii. 28. I know hundreds and thousands who have given an intellectual assent to these Divine assurances, but not many who have appropriated them in the heart. To-day, if my darling son were here, he would be twenty-one. I am commemorating his attainment of his majority; his possession of the property prepared for him from the foundation of the world.

XIII.

PATIENT WAITING.

"They shall not be ashamed that wait for me."— Is. xlix. 23.

"In the furnace God may prove thee,
Thence to bring thee forth more bright,—
But can never cease to love thee:
Thou art precious in His sight."

I HAVE this moment read your note of the 26th and cannot repress the appeal to our beloved Jesus; What am I, dear Lord, and what is my Father's house? And whence is this grace to me, that I should be permitted this sweet and exalted relation to these beloved unseen friends? Yes indeed, I will pray for you both, and with all my soul, that Jesus will manifest Himself to you; that He will fill your souls with adoring love and praise, and so draw you to Himself that you will gladly comply with the exhortation I was reading this morning, Romans, xii. 1, and I will pray Him to enable you so thoroughly to give, surrender, and dedicate yourselves to Him, that there shall remain no hindrance to His entering with all His train, and so filling these temples with His love and with His glory, that you might more easily doubt of the sun and daylight on this unclouded morning. Do not think that all these preparatory endeavors of yours, seemingly futile, are so in fact. Nothing can be farther from the truth. "Blessed are they that hunger and thirst." That, even now, is your blessedness, and not one of your aspirations is lost. "My God shall supply all your need, according to His riches in glory by Christ Jesus." It is soul refreshing to know that He will do all things in His best time. Every aspiration of yours enlarges your capacity to receive, and at the same time greatly endears you to Him. No words can adequately express the pleasure you give Him when you come lovingly and trustfully to Him expecting great things. Surely it is not difficult for you to comprehend how this may be. Here is a friend: the Friend of all friends, whose chief ground of complaint against us is, that we do not trust Him; who is ever looking to "find faith on the earth;" who searches as with a candle for confiding hearts; who most evidently values love as you and I value it: He comes to you and begs your love, your trust your undoubting confidence in Him as being in truth the loving friend He declares Himself to be. Now you experience a difficulty in immediately complying. Whence comes it? It comes of chronic worldly-mindedness,—shall I say? No, not in the sense of pleasure-loving, dancing, feasting, opera-going, dressing and utter vanity, because that is not your temptation. But I might say, chronic conventionalism; a long continued contentment with customary religiousness   Now our Lord has infused into your soul a sense of the fitness of just loving Him with all your heart. There is that in you which of late is forever saying, "Yes, that is it; that I must have; it is eminently reasonable; nothing less shall satisfy me." And that, be assured, you will attain. There is not, in my mind, a shadow of a question that you will. But it is a work of time. If some fond mother should bring you her daughter, a good and promising child of ten years, and say to you: "Mrs. G., I want you should take my child and fit her for the highest and most useful sphere in life, in a week, a month, or a year;" you would be compelled to reply: " My dear madam, you know not what you ask. It is a thing impossible in the nature of the case. Your child's mind requires time, as well as books. My business is simply to lead the way, assisting in the development of the powers which God has given her. You may count on my letting none of these suffer from neglect. Whatever talent reveals itself shall receive the most judicious encouragement."

You see the bearing of this; you may count with absolute confidence upon our Lord's tender interest in you, and care for you; and that He will put you forward as fast as you have strength to go. And His attention to your needs is not to be judged of by any sensation; nor is your progress under His tuition to be measured either by any particular sensation, or by any general complacency in any visible improvement you may think you discover in yourself. Not that you may not in fact discover in yourself such improvement as may justly impel you to give thanks to God; but, that after all, the chief occasion for grateful acknowledgment is His promise: "Ask, and ye shall receive. Whatsoever ye shall ask in my name, that will I do;" and that His Spirit makes this real to you. Here is the solid ground; the rock, standing on which, you can neither be unduly exalted by any sensible fervors, nor depressed by any diminution of emotional sensibility. It is not apparent how you could come into full possession of what I am here attempting to intimate to you, except through repeated experiences of apparent gain and loss in your spiritual husbandry. Gradually the conviction and realization will gain upon you, that Jesus is unchangeably your friend, quite irrespective of your ebb and flow of feeling, of the ups and downs of your spiritual life. Is it wonderful that the most sensitive instrument of which we have any knowledge should be greatly affected by atmospheric changes, by things visible and audible, and by things invisible and inaudible? Eph. vi. 12: "For we wrestle not with flesh and blood," etc.

XIV.

FAITH'S POWER.

"And all things whatsoever ye shall ask in prayer believing, ye shall receive."— MATT. xxi. 22.

"O Word! O dear and gentle Word!
  Thy creatures kneel before Thee,
And in ecstasies of timid love
  Delightfully adore Thee.

"O marvelous! O worshipful!
  No song or sound is heard,
But everywhere, and every hour,
In love, in wisdom, and in power,
The Father speaks His dear Eternal Word!"

I HAVE been following you with earnest intercessions in aid of your own petition and that of your unknown friend. That God has had regard to our mutual and united prayers, admits of no doubt. I have been thinking much to-day of our Lord's own testimony, as recorded by His beloved John (xiv. 12–27). Let us go over it anew. "Verily, verily, I say unto you, He that believeth on me, the works that I do, shall he do also; and greater works than these shall he do, because I go unto my Father." An unspiritual mind may doubtless weaken the force of this wonderful assurance; may limit it to the promise of miraculous powers;

or, rather, may attempt to do so. For the attempt must utterly fail, because, in the first place, a miracle being an arrest of usual laws, one miracle is as great as another. Secondly, if, for the argument's sake, we shall admit that it is more to give Lazarus again all his powers, than to give Bartimeus only sight, we may say, very well, Jesus gave Lazarus all; and in the nature of the case there can be no greater miracle than that. If Jesus fed five thousand men with a few loaves, he could as easily feed five hundred thousand with the same. And moreover, in point of fact, no disciple has ever performed miracles greater than Jesus did. So that kind of works could not be His meaning. What kind of work it was, is to be inferred from His concluding remark and reason or cause assigned: "because I go to the Father." We have His own direct statement of one of the consequences of His going to the Father (John xvi. 7), namely, that the Comforter should come. We have also information of the effect of His coming. "He shall teach you all things; He shall testify of me; He shall guide you into all truth; He shall make intercession for you with groanings that cannot be uttered. He shall be the Spirit of power." Now I can have no doubt that our Lord meant to declare his purpose, to reward the faith of each disciple with greater results in the conversion of men to God than had been seen. In strict keeping with this view is his next declaration: "And whatsoever ye shall ask in my name, that will I do, that the Father may be glorified in the Son. If ye shall ask anything in my name, I will do it." Surely this is an immense promise, and at the first glimpse it seems incredible. But two thoughts come to our relief, and to our assurance, namely, First, that that which is to be done, is to be done by the Father, for the glory of his Son, and of Himself, in his Son, and in this view nothing can be too great. Thus if it be for Christ's glory that you should at once attain that vision of Him which you so covet, then may you fearlessly ask and certainly receive it. Secondly, that the very condition, rightly understood, utterly precludes the gift of anything but that which it is best should be given, namely, "whatsoever ye shall ask in my name." How strange it seems that so many miss the force of this condition and limitation. Suppose I should go down to New Haven and ask something of your mother in your name, I being a stranger and unknown to her. What would be implied? Would not this, at least, that the giving of the thing asked should be in accordance with your interest? Also that the use I proposed to make of it, could that be known, should harmonize with your interests.

I must think that the controlling desire and endeavor in all things to please Jesus, covers the whole ground of solicitude. Especially if with this you connect the great principle of "justification by faith alone, without the deeds of the law." Does this need any words? I presume not; and yet, illustrations, which are abundant and at hand, sometimes contribute to make assurance doubly sure. For example: If I love you with all my heart, if I am pervaded with loving faith in you, I shall certainly do all the deeds, and say all the words which would be demanded by perfect obedience to the highest and strictest law. But, what would endear me to you, and satisfy your wish as respects the law, would not be the compliance with the law, but the love. Only keep in mind that you are justified by faith alone, and that your works are no otherwise of value except as they are the consistent and inseparable accompaniment of your loving confidence, — that is, faith, — and all will be well. But here is a matter about which I am concerned for you: I am afraid of your tending so strongly towards a critical surveying, weighing, and measuring everything you do, or say, or think, as to lose all freedom. Do we need any illustration to mark this danger? Suppose that in your society I should be so anxious to please you as never to have a particle of mental rest or peace. Would that be well or wise? Another point: you quote the lady who said "the world would be a blank to her, without Christ in it." And you are disturbed because you could not say that. Now I am impelled to ask if you remember what was said of certain persons in days gone by: "comparing themselves among themselves, they are not wise."

You may have experiences and expressions proper to yourself, equally acceptable to Jesus, which the lady referred to could not claim. I am not sure that I could take in the conception of "the world without Christ in it." I am not used to any such conception; it does not appear to me natural. I will venture to say, you never had any other conception of the world but as filled and pervaded by Jesus; for you have always known and acted on the knowledge that "all things were created by Him and for Him." I don't doubt your friend meant, or thought she meant, a strong, as well as a right expression; but I very much doubt if the fact she conjured up would be much if at all more foreign to her feelings than to yours. A good many strong expressions spring from peculiarities of temperament, or of thought, or of lack of thought. An array of unusual words astounds us, it may be less from any truth actually contained in them, than from the power of suggestion which unwonted words contain. Be yourself. Do not even try to be Mrs. Blank. Dr. Skinner once told me a capital story of an old father in the ministry, a Dr. Lyman Beecher kind of man, who felt himself almost annihilated by a very solemn Father Blair. Father Lyman — so I will call him — entertained Father Blair for a week. Beholding day by day this embodiment of solemnity, and contrasting with it his own untrammeled buoyancy of spirit, and freedom of utterance, he felt, as he said, that he had no piety at all. It was his custom every Saturday afternoon to meet his elders and pray and confer with them in the little schoolroom contiguous to his church. He was remarkable for his punctuality to all his engagements. But when Saturday came, the assembled elders eyed the clock and wondered at his non-appearance. Ten minutes past, fifteen, twenty, then the minister was seen coming across the green. But in what unwonted guise! The horse which before never lacked abundant hints to hasten, was now creeping along; his rider not now erect, but drooping. Solemnly the old man dismounted; slowly and solemnly he tied his nag. Solemnly he took his seat and said never a word. The senior elder, after a brief pause demanded, "Parson, are you sick?" "No." "Is your wife sick?" "No." "Has anything happened?" "No." "Well, then, you're clean daft." "Well, I believe I am. I can't be Father Blair, and it's no use to try. Brethren, we'll proceed to business," and at it he went in his old natural style.

You do not know how you would feel under the loss of any friend, until the loss comes. Much less can you even imagine, ever so faintly, what it would be to have it really brought home to your conviction, that Jesus was no longer in the world. Neither do I believe you have any call to attempt to work yourself up to the ecstasy of any brother or sister, be he or she more or less fervent in prayer or in speech. Ask the Holy One to touch your lips and heart with a coal from off His altar, and He will do it. No matter whether the result compares with Mrs. A.'s or Mrs. B.'s experience. You may be no more like Mrs. A. or Mrs. B. than a peach is like a pumpkin. You were not made to do their work, but your own. There is more than an even chance that the idea of "almost touching Jesus," would send your mind off in a totally wrong direction. Drop that, and do not look for that, but look directly to Him, and take what comes from Him. Oh, to be totally disabused of groundless and materialistic anticipations! Ask Him as freely as you will, and take all from Him. Let Him come near to you in His own way. It is a hundred to one that He will come to you in a way for which you have found no precedent. That was my own experience in "finding God real." No Mrs. A. or Mrs. B. ever told me that. Jesus revealed Himself to me, manifested Himself, and so manifested Himself, that I knew Him, and rejoiced in Him.

As to "entering into the enjoyment of your friends, in that prayer-meeting, to the extent they did," much might be said. Premising that it certainly does not look favorable for the spiritual condition of any of us, to be found without sensibility to any increase of genuine spiritual fervor, I may declare to you, as the combined result of experience and observation, that few things are more misleading than sensible fervors. I have many a time been completely extinguished by the astonishing fervors of persons — comparing my own love with theirs, it seemed to me to be nothing — whom I found to be neither truthful nor honest. Others there were whose fervors soon burned out, and the persons subsided into a rate of living which compelled serious doubt whether they ever had any fire of true devotion. Meanwhile I found my own love had not only suffered no abatement, but had gone on increasing, through summer's heat and winter's cold, quite independent of what others might, or might not, be feeling, saying, or doing. I could write a volume under this head. I have sat under the utterance of vehement remarks as to what prayer ought to be, until I was filled with a sense of the impossibility of praying at all after such a prelude. Again, I have been asked to join a little circle for occasional prayer by a person whose spiritual life was to me a mystery and a contradiction of everything suitable and reasonable. Often and often have I wondered how this good man could travel round like a horse a in very small mill, saying always, 'Brethren, what we want is to be stirred up." Often my inward response was, "Brother, there is nothing to stir up." Our need was of fresh supplies of Divine truth and Divine love. Often have I felt, I cannot pray to any purpose, in the wake of one whose soul knows so little of quiet peace in believing. I think the feeling that you must, and that you ought to be thus and thus affected by what you hear, sometimes effectually steels one against all right feeling. To sit meekly at the feet of Jesus, and learn patiently of Him, and of Him alone, is surely one of the least common attainments found here below. Of course I do not for a moment mean to imply that we may not learn all we can from our fellow Christians. But I think there is a temptation, not uncommon, to insist upon church-members heating-up, if the expression can be pardoned, under fervid appeals from one another. I have nothing at all to say against the use of a genuine power to arouse and benefit others by any honored possessor of this power, but the eloquence of truth, God's truth, dropping ever so quietly into a mind always offered to the occupancy of the Comforter, — oh, how superior is this! And how much more enduring the inspirations thus received, than those heats which appear to consist with frequent and most reprehensible irregularities, even to suspension of spiritual life.

I greatly enjoyed my Bible classes on Saturday evening, on Sabbath morning, on Monday evening, and on Tuesday afternoon. What a variety of experiences I have had in these same classes! Sometimes such a lack of physical strength; such an almost impossibility at times of obtaining any freedom in prayer for them. But this winter all that is changed. I seem to have strength and to spare. Praying is as easy as breathing; and what is more wonderful for me, breathing is as easy as praying. And yet I cannot talk of these great expectations, which I have often heard expressed. I have simply an unwavering confidence that Jesus will bestow abundant fruit of this labor, but no ability to single out the individuals in whom it will be found.

XV.

PEACEFUL LOVE.

John xiv. 27: "Peace I leave with you, my peace I give unto you." xv. 9: "As the Father hath loved me, so have I loved you: continue ye in my love." xiv. 21: "And I will manifest myself to you."

> "On wind-swept ponds the lilies rest,
>   And yield their sweet perfume;
> The surface hold nor e'er distrest
>   By rise or fall of wave or moon.
> So with the soul that's stayed on God;
>   Rooted in depths unseen of men,
> His peace is like a river broad,
>   His rest beyond all human ken.
>
> "His skies are starred with God's commands;
>   And these are mirrored in his soul;
> From heights and depths he lifts his hands
>   And prays to Him who made the whole:
> 'Take all my will, but leave me Thine,
>   Redeem Thy pledge, Thyself reveal,
> For Thou art truly, surely, mine,
>   And I await Thy love, Thy seal.'" — Eph. i. 13.

YOU are kind enough to speak of my being useful to you, but you have little idea how useful you are to me. I feel sure that you and your unknown friend have been praying for me this morning, from the uncommonly sweet and peaceful communion with our precious Lord I have been enjoying. I thank you with all my heart. I have been entreating Him to bestow the same serene peace on each of you. I like to pray for my friends by name. Our beloved brother Paul used and enjoyed that privilege. And if you will earnestly pray by name for those in whose usefulness our Lord Jesus has interested you, such earnest praying will certainly greatly help your endeavors to see Jesus. Such praying is real coöperation with Him, and when persisted in, must needs make real and present to you, Him with whom you thus co-labor.

You ask, "Is it wrong to indulge the thought that Jesus planned what gives you pleasure and profit?" Pardon me, but I cannot help exclaiming, how almost infinitely small must be the measure of loving trust in Him, that permits you to ask such a question! Indeed, I do not mean to give you pain, but how can you, who are so quick to discern even the slightest indication of the painstaking of loving friends, how can you for a moment hesitate to recognize the loving painstaking of Jesus, who loves you so much more?

Upon another point you unquestionably deceive yourself, I think. You say, "If only I could say truly that I entered into this matter with all my soul, I should be content." Now please tell me, or rather, tell yourself, what you mean by "all your soul." Doubtless you are not vehemently excited. But no more are you about your husband, or about your mother. And yet I have no doubt you love each of these with all your heart. Then vehement excitement is not necessarily the only type of all-the-soul interest. Doubtless your love to your husband is, among other ways, to be measured in this way: by your steady, continuous, persistent endeavors to promote his interests, and to forward his usefulness, with a measure of feeling appropriate to the demand of each day's work. Now when you add that "you think you can sincerely say, that it is the honest desire of your heart to be thoroughly emptied of self, and conformed to the will of God," you appear to me to come right up to the condition of the test I seek to apply. I am very glad of what you are enabled to say about being "pure in heart." That beatitude is inexpressibly sweet to me: "Blessed are the pure in heart, for they shall see God." I have sometimes lived on that verse for a long time. It seems to me the sweetest thing in the world to be; as loving Jesus is the sweetest thing to do. And clearly they are so inseparably related, that the one is the condition of the other.

When you "get bewildered," lean on Jesus. You have read Miss Fidelia Fiske's narrative of the poor Nestorian woman and remember her whispered "If you love me lean hard." Was ever anything sweeter than this! When I read it I thought of Jesus — heard His voice in it, and the tears would not hold back. When you are bewildered, if you love Him, lean hard on Jesus; and remember, — oh, how many times it has relieved me inexpressibly to remember it, — "I have got only one thing tc do at a time." Remember also, that, "In the Lord Jehovah is everlasting strength." This assurance has been worth more than a mine of gold to me. I find in it a wonderful and infinitely varied application to every variety of solicitude, care, and anxiety. It is an expansion of, and a commentary upon, that other brief prescription: "Be careful for nothing." Never yield place in your heart to a fever of anxiety about anything. Has He not laid in Zion a foundation for this restful trust? "a stone, a tried stone, a precious corner-stone, a sure foundation?"

Do you own "Christ Our Example, By Caroline Fry, With Autobiography Prefixed"? It appears to me one of the best books in the whole range of religious literature; sound, earnest, admirably written, discriminating, full of instruction and encouragement, a sweet example of the noblest Christian life.

How plain it is, from the narrative of your mental and heart struggles about this call to M., that God has heard your prayers for sanctification! Is not this the history of the saints from long before the time of John Newton? Often have I felt convinced that in daring to "seek first the kingdom of God and his righteousness," I have laid my dearest friends under the same liability to discipline to which my prayer and endeavor exposes me. Here is your husband, very probably suffering under the discipline of suspense and mental conflict because you have been hungering and thirsting after righteousness. Not but that the Divine wisdom finds a needs be and a benefit in it all for him too, as truly as though he alone were the object of God's care. Hardly anything brings to me so often an affecting illustration of the wonderful extent of our Lord's resources as the perception that He can carry on the education of two, or of twenty, souls as easily as that of one; and moreover that He can and does provide that the discipline which primarily is for one, is equally in place for the other; and still again that the suffering of one, sympathized in and shared by the other, shall be the precise thing most needful and useful for that other. When I think of all this, I am overwhelmed, and can only exclaim, "Who is sufficient for all these things! It is as high as heaven; what canst thou do? Deeper than hell; what canst thou know?" You say, "If through failure to seek earnestly enough, importunately enough, we have been permitted to make a mistake!" Stop a moment, and think of Jesus' words: "My peace I leave with you; my peace I give unto you;" and think of what hangs thereby. Anxious importunity may well have its place in the transition state from chronic unbelief in the Divine guidance, to simple, affectionate, loving trust. But to you, who have now long known that Jesus has sent the Comforter; that He dwells with you and in you; that He constantly guides you; how proper is that serene trust which rejoices in knowing that He has promised guidance; that He abideth faithful; that He never will, that He cannot leave you or forsake you. My dear friend, see Jesus in all this, actually leading, guiding, keeping you, and rest calmly in the profound, undisturbed, undoubting conviction, that He who said, "I will guide thee with mine eye," has done and is doing so. You will be assisted in this, by just falling back upon His own testimony: "So God made man in His own image." Consider how we value a stable, peaceful trust in ourselves and in each other after the friendly intercourse between us which has existed for a few months only. I certainly should feel grieved if you should write me in a flutter of doubt and anxious concern, lest a slip of your pen, an unguarded expression, a mistake, more or less, in one form or another, would jeopard all the love I bear you, alienate my friendly regards, and provoke me to leave you to go wrong, when it was in my power to point out for you the true way. You would not so distrust me. Is it not abundantly plain that you ought not to conceive of it as a possibility that Jesus would leave you, His disciple and friend, and your husband, His called and commissioned minister, to err, for the lack of greater vehemence of importunity? Does not quiet confidence, and soul refreshing rest in His promise of guidance, and in His love, more honor Him, as well as contribute immensely more to your happiness, and so to your power to inspire in others like precious faith?

Of course "you have both been led to a more earnest consecration of yourselves to the service of the Master." That is just what He aimed at when he moved the M. people to open the subject of your removal. And what He aims at, He secures. Is it not most blessed to think, aye, and to know, so as irrepressibly to shout, with our beloved brother Paul, "I am persuaded that neither death, nor life, nor angels, nor principalities, nor powers, nor things present, nor things to come, nor height nor depth, nor any other creature," not even a call from M. nor the decision thereupon, "shall be able to separate us from the love of God which is in Christ Jesus our Lord." That was my last lesson in my beloved Tuesday class; and I enjoyed the assurance to the uttermost. And the last lesson in the Monday evening class mated well with it: "I am the bread of life." I felt profoundly and with entire delight how Jesus is to the soul, what bread is to the body. Tell your good husband to keep up a brave heart, and never doubt that the Comforter led him to the right decision.

I could not forbear a pleased smile when I came to your disappointment because Mr. —— thrust himself upon you; and your question, "Did God order that?" You are learning. Yes, God did order that. How many times I have asked myself just that question: "Shall there be evil in a city, and the Lord hath not done it?" Can any chance thrust itself upon, and defeat His plan? No indeed! But that is not the whole of the case. If you are at all like me, you will understand me when I say, that I want to apply remedies, and achieve all other things, in about three minutes. Now I do not feel that Jesus blames me for that; but He desires and intends to show me a more excellent way. He means that I shall completely comprehend that He holds all hearts in His hand. He means that we shall be schooled to a full appreciation of the origin of every blessing; that it is "not of ourselves, but the gift of God." Hundreds and hundreds of times have I been over this ground. There is for all things a best time. Doubtless He who gave man knowledge, knew that that ride in the cars about which conscience troubles you, was not the best time for the purpose. Nor was that all. He had this lesson for you, which He sends me to deliver: "My dear child, begin with a deeper realization of my tender interest in your friend N. She is graven upon the palms of my hands; she is dear to me as the apple of the eye; I have hidden her under the shadow of my wings. She, dear child, does not know it; but it is true, none the less. A mother may forget her infant, but I cannot forget N. You shall have the privilege of helping her; I love you for wishing it; but not to-day. I would have you accustom yourself yet more to the sense of my timeliness. I do all things in the best time.

I shall not explain to you why to-day is not the best time. I accept your will to serve. Trust me. For your good; for the trial of your faith, I may see fit to hold this case before you, as a study, for a long time, showing you a lovely and superior person continued under the limiting and depressing influence of great disabilities. If you think this will be very hard for her; let me remind you that such was the life of thy Lord from the beginning to the close; a life of suffering for the benefit of others. Is it nothing for her that she is permitted to walk in my foot-prints? to share my experiences?"

Thus, it seems to me, he reasons with you about your solicitude for N. Such an one I have in my Tuesday class. If your friend ever visits Hartford persuade her to take the friendly advice of Dr. B. A great many cases of religious trouble need medical advice from an intelligent Christian physician, who can trace the distress to its origin, often a physical malady. I have a dear friend, one of the most useful ministers in the Presbyterian Church, who by a preparation of iron, administered by Dr. B., was raised from the depths of religious depression, to a health, vigor, and executive power that any of us might envy. To N., some day, it may be well to say, Now admit that your case is chronic and irremediable. You are a suffering child of God and are to continue so. It is His will. Can you not accept the bitter cup from His hands, and for His sake drink it? He drained the bitter cup for thee. Doubtless, as He appointed it, He sees the painful road you travel, to be the safe road. Ask of Him grace to accept His appointment, and strength to rest in His will.

XVI.

REAL PRAYER.

> "Pray and believe, for God is true;
> Trust, and receive His love for you;
> Thy warrant is, that He has spoken;
> His uttered word can ne'er be broken."

"THEN shall you know, if you follow on to know the Lord." That is my answer to your "wonder if you know anything about real prayer." I have no doubt whatever that you do already know much about it. But how large the sphere of prayer is! And how much, even to the most advanced, ever remains to be known. It is not, however, the knowledge of prayer, which is for the moment so much a question with you. It is rather the knowledge of Jesus, whom you have failed to find real, personal, near, and very dear to you.

The postman who brought me your letter, brought another from the friend you quote as "being so absorbed in Jesus that she forgot herself totally, sins and all." Now that friend, when the Master first sent her to me, only two years ago, was, though a church-member, as nearly as possible a total skeptic. Her father, grandfather, and great grandfather, "back to the time whereunto the memory of man runneth not to the contrary," were all skeptics. A year or more ago, when I was pressing the necessity of loving Jesus as she loved her mother, she replied, that "that was out of the question, for she had been accustomed to go to her mother all her life, with everything, and had been counseled and comforted by her times innumerable; and so of course she could not love Jesus as she loved her mother!" I admitted, that so long as she put Jesus at that disadvantage, it would continue impossible. But how, I said, if you were to give Jesus His own place — the place He claims, — and go always first of all to Him with everything? Would He not then prove Himself to be as kind? aye, and an infinitely more tender as well as an infinitely wiser friend? And now I trust she has found it so. Be frank with our dear Redeemer, our beloved Lord. Tell Him everything, and the day is not distant when you will cease questioning "whether you know anything of real prayer." I was much pleased in reading your question, "Don't you think God is sometimes better pleased with the sacrifice we make in not doing a thing, than He would be with the deed?" Indeed I do. Thousands of times that has been my only comfort. For example, when I was writing "Heaven." I was a long, long time about it. Hundreds of times when my mind was in prime working order, when the whole region of thought seemed thrown wide open to view, I was compelled to recognize as His will, and my duty, to lay down the pen, and go about these streets proving and disproving to earn money. Nothing but the love of Jesus, and the supreme desire to please Him, could have made me acquiescent; for I knew, from oft repeated experience, that when the hour of respite from business came, the region of thought and of sentiment would be shrouded in shadow.

You say, "you do not doubt that there is such a thing as communion with God." A word or two about that. On God's part, He speaks to you in the Bible. I hope you have adopted, and are acting upon the rule never to begin to read that, till you have first asked the Holy Spirit to guide you in the reading; to enable you to realize your present Lord, uttering His message, and also to take gladly and with fervent thanks His message to your heart. Your description of what "all the soul," includes, is most just, but I hope you will not forget that "we have this treasure in earthern vessels," and that we are not to write bitter things against ourselves because we do not invariably come up to that. "He knoweth our frame; He remembereth that we are dust." It wanted quarter to twelve last night when I finished the letter to M. D., and I thought of my darling James, saying within myself, What an honor it will be, if I can wear out as he did, in the Master's service.

Not that I have any intention of doing any imprudent thing, if I know it to be such. Nor did James know that preaching bareheaded on the open plain before Nashville was perilous. No, I mean to get the very utmost work out of this body and soul that the most cool-blooded calculation can show to be practicable; recognizing, of course, that this must include the friction, upon an emergency, of running now and then a fast train.

XVII.

BARRENNESS.

"What time I am afraid, I will trust in Thee."— Ps. lvi. 3.

" Take courage, then, my trembling soul;
One look from Christ will make thee whole;
Trust thou in Him, 't is not in vain,
But wait and look, — and look again!"

YOU are hasty in your conclusion that " I never have any such days, — days in which prayer seems utterly impossible." "There hath no temptation taken you, but such as is common to man." It is a trial of your faith which I know only too well. It does not, however, appal me as it once did. I have had seasons, almost every year, lasting from three or four days, to nearly as many months, in which " neither sun nor stars appeared." It was an intellectual obscuration. I seemed to have no power to fix my thoughts on God or divine things, and was as void of all feeling as a stone. Now if one depends at all on frames and feelings, such an experience brings dismay. On the other hand, if one has learned just to look up and say, Lord Jesus, I am Thine, whether in sunshine or in shadow; with comfort or without, I shall go steadily on doing what I think to be acceptable to Thee; then faith grows, even as the grass grows in the night. The time will come when you will thank our dear Jesus for this too. You have no need to refer it to ill health; nor need you infer, as an inevitable conclusion, that you have lost ground. Refer it to His good-will, and find in it the evidence that He has set His heart on your sanctification. Were you always to have the fervor and fluency you sometimes have, you might mistake what in a thousand instances comes of mere animal spirits, for pure spiritual life. At such times of privation one gets excellent opportunities for faithful and sensible self-examination. Thus we inquire, Do I wish to turn to any other for life, light, or joy? Am I any less bent on serving my Lord? Can I not truly, and with emphasis, say, "Whom have I in heaven but Thee? And there is none upon earth I desire beside Thee." Am I not more ready than ever to exclaim, "If I forget Thee, let my right hand forget her cunning; let my tongue cleave to the roof of my mouth, if I prefer not Thee before my chief joy."

Suppose "one does make a little slip, or omit a duty here or there," it does not follow that "one loses so much ground that it is discouraging to try to think of recovering it." What one is apt to lose is, self-complacency. And it is, to be sure, vexing, just when we were ready to think that we were becoming pretty good, to be reminded that all the apparent improvement has oozed out through a flaw in the vessel. Now the real improvement is seen in the stubbornness of the resolve we immediately adopt: "Well, if I never succeed, I will keep on trying till the end of time." "By patient continuance in well-doing," not by sensible fervors excited by conscious progress, we "shall inherit glory, honor, and immortality." Now I know you too well to have any fear that you will be offended by my plain dealing. Nor do I believe you will really adopt any such rash resolution, as that "you will not write me again." Instead of that, I want you to accept and use one of two prescriptions, according to your preference. If you cleave to the old practice, get a handful of camomile flowers and make a tea from some of them, to be drank cold, say a third of a tumbler, three mornings in succession, before breakfast. If homœopathic treatment has your preference, then take five drops of nux in a spoonful of water before each meal, for a day or two, and I shall be disappointed if you do not find yourself more hopeful. I wonder if any good friend ever suggested to you your duty to be as patient with yourself as you would with another, and allow time to correct all that needs correction? "The trial of your faith is much more precious than of gold that perisheth;" and you will come upon a solid and enduring foundation when you shall have adopted the habit of referring every manner of trial to the hand — to the heart, too — of the Refiner and Purifier, who means to present you in Zion perfect before God. Take the case of our dear N., — I say our, because we have a common property in all saints, though unseen, unknown in person, — "All things are yours," — and in this case peculiarly, because we have together prayed for her. I say, take her case and apply the principle, ascribing all discipline to Jesus. There are, most unquestionably, loving reasons, why He has dealt and is dealing with her in this painful way. On our part, it is alike a duty and a privilege to attempt to our utmost to alleviate her sad condition. But I have found many cases more or less resembling Cowper's, which He has permitted to continue unalleviated for years. I think such cases demand of us an undoubting faith in the wisdom and the goodness of our Lord. It is too common to dispose of them by referring their origin merely to second causes; to sickness, etc., etc. But that is want of faith. Shall any one of His disciples be ailing, and the Lord hath not done it? "When Jesus knew that Lazarus was sick, He abode two days still in the same place where he was." Here is a lesson for us. There was then something better than that Lazarus should get well. So to-day, there is, for the time being, something better than that dear N. should be well. Doubtless the Lord is dealing with that rebelliousness of hers. Meanwhile it is ours to pray and watch. Have faith in God, for yourself, and for N., and remember it is no matter how "it seems." "In all these things we are more than conquerors through Him that loved us."

XVIII.

JESUS' TENDERNESS.

"Like as a father pitieth his children, so the Lord pitieth them that fear Him." — Ps. ciii. 13.

"His heart is made of tenderness —
It melts with pitying love."

"And as feeble babes that suffer,
Toss and cry, and will not rest,
Are the ones the tender mother
Holds the closest, loves the best,
So when we are weak and wretched,
By our sins weighed down, distressed,
Then it is that God's great patience
Holds us closest, loves us best."

THERE is one thing you fail to do, and it is a very serious failure. You fail to give our dear Lord Jesus credit for loving-tenderness. Even with the very little reason I have given you to recognize something of that in me, I should probably think it hard if you treated me as you treat Him. You cloak it, indeed, in part, under your strong disapprobation of yourself. But, you are bound to consider, not merely what is due to your unworthiness, but also what is due from Himself to Himself. Now He owes it to his own sweet nature to compassionate and help the weak and erring. He ever acts on that obligation. You do not give Him credit for it. He owes it to His own infinite wisdom and to His no less infinite power to do always the best thing; and He always does that. You are bound to think of what is due to Him three times for every once that you pore over your own ill desert. When you do this, you will fall to praising, as you ought. You magnify your failures out of all proportion to their actual importance. This is very plausible, but it will not stand the scrutiny of a close examination. True humility cannot be blind to the number and magnitude of its blessings. It will break out in recognizing acknowledgments: Whence is this grace of my God to me! Oh, how canst Thou thus overwhelm with Thy blessing one who is so unworthy? Dear Lord, my praise is all unworthy of Thine acceptance, but, poor as it is, I must praise Thee, or the very stones will cry out. Yesterday my faculties were shrouded in fog. I had to take doses of paregoric; nothing serious, only a cold which had got hold somewhere in the system, and brought with it surges of pain like the roll of the incoming sea. This morning when I came down the fog was all gone, and I thought of you as I looked up to dear Jesus, and just luxuriated in thinking how good and wise He is, and blessed and adored Him and I wished you might have the same serene enjoyment in communion with Him. It was no effort at all to praise and pray. One of my dear sons was asking me last evening, what He must do to become a Christian.

"Only love Jesus as you do your mother," I said, "and give yourself to Him."

"I've tried and tried to give myself to Him, and nothing comes of it."

"How do you know that? You might as well say, I've tried and tried to get an education, and nothing comes of it. You never try to do right, but something comes of it. Whether you see it, is another question. Your business is to try and try again. God will see, if you ask in Jesus' name, that something shall come of it." Why don't you lay down your head on Jesus' bosom? You are as welcome to this as to the air you breathe?

Still you sigh, "Oh, that I could realize Jesus!" Well, dear friend, take a lesson from the wisest of men: "If the iron is dull, put to the strength." If you have blunted faith through disuse, strive to put new vigor into it though strength of will. Be it that faith is the gift of God: I say, so much the better; for He will surely give it to one who is firmly resolved on possessing it.

You ask me to expound a verse. I would rather first expound for you that other verse, "Beloved, if our heart condemn us not, then have we confidence toward God." Here is the illustration: I am a friend of yours. I come to your house with all the laws of polite intercourse fixed in my mind: "Thou shalt do this;" "thou shalt not do that." I might keep to all these rules, and have a weary time of it. But, as George Herbert tersely says,

> "How wide is all this long pretense!
> There is in love a sweetness ready penned;
> Copy out only that, and save expense."

If I love you in my heart, I may or may not keep fully up to the rules; love will set me at ease. My heart will assure me of my loyalty to you, and I shall have confidence in your love for me. Is not that plain? Now I am ready for the verse you propose. If our Lord finds a loving heart in you, He will not condemn you. If He finds you, in a legal spirit relying, or trying to rely, on your obedience to rules without love in your heart, He will find you wanting. Is not that it?

"When you can't do anything," you are required patiently to accept that disability, and be content to let some one else do it. "They also serve who only stand and wait." I have had to accept this prescription many a time. But even this thing is one of the "all things," that work together for good to them that love God. Indeed, no man's dross can be purely purged without the refining fire of this particular discipline. I know there is a possibility of sinking into supineness; less perhaps for such temperaments as ours, than for some others. Our discipline seems to be to keep balancing questions.

That, though very uncomfortable, may be not unprofitable. It has been like a guiding star to me to remember, that Jesus having said, "My yoke is easy and my burden is light," it is my business to find it as He states it. Not to find it so, is to have somewhere failed of due attention to the terms of His service, and I must go back, searching each step of my way till the misstep is found. I have often had occasion to think, there cannot be in all the world one so utterly dependent as I, upon immediate and ever renewed Divine help. Some men have genius, original endowments, upon which they can count in the day of need. I have absolutely nothing, but as He gives from hour to hour. For two months I have been wishing to write a few lines for our paper, but not a word could I write till yesterday, and in that word I have no confidence. Often and often it seems to me I shall never again write a word of any use to anybody. There is no other way for us, but to face in the right direction, and wait for marching orders. When the order comes, He will give the power to move. Your referring to Peter brings back an occurrence of yesterday. Our little six-year old was found by Mrs. K. looking for a Testament. The little one sat an hour reading it. When mother returned to the parlor, she said, "See here, mamma, Peter went out and wept bitterly. When I read such stories as that, it makes tears come in my eyes. And he said he would not deny Jesus, mamma, but he did." Have you a doubt that this little one had been putting her abortive endeavors to keep good resolutions along with Peter's? Or that she had a fellow-feeling with him?

XIX.

WEIGHING EVIDENCE.

"My soul, wait thou only upon God, for my expectation is from Him." —
PSALM lxii. 5.

"O foolish man! where are thine eyes?
How hast thou lost them in a crowd of cares."

THERE must be a limit to our questioning; some point at which, in a case calling for decision, we must come to a decision. I know not how, in our courts of law, there could ever be an adjudication, if a point were never reached at which it should be ruled that "the evidence is all in." When that point is reached, the advocate is permitted to make the best showing he can, — on the one side, and on the other, — and then the jury give their conclusion on the evidence. It seems to me that you have gone over just this ground. And I see not why you should not accept the result as the decision of your Lord. Be it that you yourself were made judge in the case; be it that you are no exception to the truth; that human judges are liable to err. Unless conviction of error is unavoidable, it seems to me unwise, of your own motion, to disturb your decision. If a reconsideration is forced upon you,

I should say, Take it as though it were an original case, now first presented; and go into the examination with the utmost carefulness, prayerfulness, and painstaking to reach the truth. But as God Himself is settled and serene in His conclusions, so I have no doubt He desires, and has provided, as a general rule, that we in our measure shall be in ours. I do not think we are warranted to assume that Jesus never suffers His disciples to err in judgment; for our errors in judgment often furnish avenues for the admission of our most valuable lessons; lessons which rarely come home to us in any other way. I think we are authorized to believe, with the utmost confidence, that every true-hearted disciple is so guided by his Master that the conclusion reached is the conclusion most desirable for him. I should be sorry indeed to doubt this. "We are not under the law, but under grace;" and herein is the very felicity of our condition, that our Lord deals better with us than either law, or our own erring judgment, would provide. Just in proportion as you were conscious of the controlling desire to do as you thought Jesus would be best pleased to have you, in that proportion I think you were and are bound to believe that He was and is pleased with you. To indulge any other belief, is, in effect, to make void His assurance that His yoke is easy, and His burden light. For if the sincerely desirous to do right cannot know what He esteems right, then miserable suspense and self-condemnation are inevitable, and all because of the endeavor obediently to take His yoke! Further, let me answer: "the questionings," of which you speak, come of unbelief in our Lord's guidance, veiled in the plausible garb of a deep sense of our own fallibility. True, we are fallible; prone to err; but is the promise of God therefore to be made of no effect? And for whom is the promise? Is it only for the unerring? for those who have least need of it? Is it not also for those who need it most? I think that when God presents "the two sides of a question so nearly balanced that you cannot for your life tell which indicates the path of duty," the point at which He aims is less the issue of the question, than the process — the use you make of the pros and the cons. I fancy the desire, evident to Him, and the pains you take to please Him, are the thing of moment and of value in His esteem. And this you seem to have contemplated when you ask, "May not one admit the possibility of a failure to make a wise decision, without distrusting God's overruling providence?" One thing is surely plain: the even balance of this question is forcing on you a closeness and a frequency of appeal to our Lord, most evidently suited to make God real to you. "Trying to rest, but every new wave drives you out to sea again;" that is, you are making the painful discovery that "an evil heart of unbelief" is an exceedingly evil heart; and that sin is indeed the evil thing God declares it to be. That is a lesson, beloved, we all have to learn, and to learn it from our own experience. There is no taking this upon the testimony of others. We may get the theory, but the painful and salutary conviction apparently can come home to us, only as you are now experiencing. So I have found it. So you find it. And finding this to be so, you can and must draw the inference that "He cares for you," and intends developing in you precisely what you are longing for, conscious love to Him. Only believe what is most palpably true, that He is doing this great and good thing for you, and in you, and how can you help growing in conscious love to Him? Again, I reply, that I do not "think it is wrong, wicked, to be so tossed about," so long as the tossing is so evidently the result of rowing against wind and tide. The "wavering" we are warned against is of quite another sort, namely, that of the man who has no such faith as impels one thus to struggle in defiance of winds and waves. Unsatisfactory as it is to yourself, I cannot doubt that you are giving far more satisfactory evidence of faith to Him, than when in the calm of unconcern to please Him.

Lately I met a clergyman to whom I said, I have a pleasant remembrance of the days when you used to come into —— Church with the old doctor, and make those fervid addresses. "Pshaw!" he replied, those were the days of my youthful inexperience," etc. To which I made answer, mentally: Alas, had you but known the things which belong to the sphere for which you were made! But having been translated to a prominent church, and bribed to adopt the notion that logic must in such quarters supplant simple fervid exhortation, you have buried the man that was, and one who adorned his profession, setting up in his place the shadow of one you were never made to be. This man as you see, acknowledged an error which was not an error, and caught at an amendment which was no amendment. And yet, even in this case, so wonderful are the compensations in the Divine economy, I dare not indulge an unqualified regret. My judgment would say, had he stuck to the humble things which he scornfully repudiated, he would probably have been eminently successful. Possibly the success might have been prejudicial to his soul. As it is, his way has been full of thorns, and the Lord who put them there, knows for what. I don't believe it is well to be very anxious about remote results. I strongly suspect our time for solicitude is, to act as well as we can, with the light we have to-day, this hour, now. It is not certain that it is a want of faith that makes you go over the matter in your mind. That may be God's will. He may make it "the fiery trial which is to try you," and purge away your dross. It may be that this is not to be avoided; that a necessity is laid upon you to review, and re-review the matter. I have already intimated one apparent reason for this, namely, to make you realize the necessity and the practicability of throwing yourself more completely on Jesus. Of this I am sure; only be earnest and loyal, and be the result what it may, the process is sure to work this blessedness for you. Can you then quarrel with your schooling? If the Lord has loosened you from E., as He has, it is for something. It may, or may not be, to remove to M.

XX.

FAITH'S SCALE.

" Now, Lord, I leave at Thy loved feet
  This thing which looks so near, so sweet;
  I will not seek, I will not long —
  I almost fear I have been wrong;
  I'll go and work the harder, Lord,
  And wait till by some loud, clear word
  Thou callest me to Thy loved feet
  To take this thing so dear so sweet."

I HAVE just taken up the eleventh Hebrews and looked through it carefully hoping to find help in answering your inquiry. Observe how it confirms what I have often said. Abel, Enoch, Noah, Abraham, Sarah, Isaac, Jacob, Joseph, Moses, and the rest of that honored roll, each and all acted upon some fact known to himself as a simple matter of faith. It is written, "These all died in faith, not having received the promises, but having seen them afar off, and were persuaded of them, and embraced them." Here, it seems to me, is the very gist of the thing. Let us apply it to yourself. You do not see Jesus with your eyes; you do not get written letters from Him; but you fully believe in Him as a true and constant friend; as present always; as arranging all your fortunes; as ordering every incident in your life, as being as simply and truly pleased by your endeavors to please, as your husband, or myself, or any friend you have. Now it seems to me, that your treating Him as thus real, and your persistent endeavors in everything to please Him, must inevitably issue as it did with Enoch: "Before he was translated he had this testimony, that he pleased God." So it must be with you; only it seems important to this result, that you should, without waiting for the testimony or for anything else, simply and at once, believe and rejoice that He is pleasable. Take the comfort of the conviction, which is fully warranted by His own language, that you do please Him.

I am quite sure that many Christians err in making their measure of success in accomplishing their endeavors, the measure of their faith and of their acceptableness to Jesus. We do not so judge of the friend who struggles against wind and stream to serve us. Of course where faith exists it will work and improve, but this improvement, in the very nature of the case is not and cannot be instantaneously complete. What then? Must we not indulge, or can we not possess joy and peace in believing? What says the Apostle Paul, speaking by the Holy Ghost? "Therefore being justified by faith, we have peace with God through our Lord Jesus Christ." Hear also John, the beloved: "Beloved, if our heart condemn us not, then have we confidence toward God." Whatever you exercise faith in Jesus for, in that you will be accepted; which is, I apprehend, the true intent of "Whatsoever ye ask believing, ye shall receive." And is not this incomparably more and better than merely receiving literally the precise thing you ask? I should be sorry to be compelled to believe that I could stand only on the literal ground; that I must ask with unerring accuracy for just what I need; that I must believe that I shall receive just that and nothing more, or other. I believe I never made a truer or more acceptable prayer than when, in 1833, I poured out my soul in this prayer: "O Lord, give me I know not what! Give me what thou seest me to need. I am sensible, deeply, painfully sensible of need; but what I need, I know not; Thou knowest. Take me, Lord, just as I am, and make me just what thou wouldst have me be, for Christ's dear sake."

You can see how this prayer necessitated faith. You can see that by placing me in this condition of extreme ignorance, He placed me in the condition most favorable to faith. I knew neither what to expect, nor when to expect it. That did not preclude, but rather predisposed to affectionate trust and childlike confidence in His ordering of events and results. You cannot but see that a childlike faith honors God more than any other thing can; and thence you derive the strongest possible argument, when you plead, "Lord, increase my faith." Just consider the absolute impossibility that the

Father will refuse anything that will honor Jesus. And consider what is implied in asking in the name of Jesus. The asking of a disciple in the interest of Jesus is Jesus' own asking. When the orderly of General Grant, goes to government for anything, it is the Commander-in-Chief who asks. True the orderly himself may be personally agreeable to the Secretary of War, but the request is that of his superior, and it comes to the government with the full force of the Commander-in-Chief's official position. So every prayer of yours, offered in the name and interest of Jesus, has the full force of the asking of God's own dear Son. In answer to your question I reply: Most assuredly your hungering, longing desire for the realized presence of Jesus, is His own gift, and an earnest, aye, an actual installment of the thing desired. " Blessed are they that hunger and thirst, for they shall be filled." Filled with what ? With just what the Lord meant by righteousness ; which in this place I have no doubt is right-ness ; that is acceptableness with Him. This is not perfection absolute, but lovableness. And what makes us lovable to Him who looks on the heart? Evidently a heart-desire to please Him. And how will the fulfillment of this promise be evidenced? By increased hunger and thirst ; so that the more God grants your petition, the more sensible will be your hunger, the more insatiable your thirst. As to "the sense of Christ's nearness," it seems to me that the direct pursuit of it, like the direct pursuit of health, often baffles the pursuer. There was a deep and sound philosophy in the answer of the child, to "What makes everybody love you?" "I don't know, unless it is because I love everybody." Loving Jesus, and trying in all things to promote His interests and wishes must inevitably result in the consciousness of His nearness and love. Clearly this is entirely another thing from legality and works of purchase. Miss D.'s quotation, "Simply a belief in Christ's words because they are His words," ought to be all-sufficient; but, unfortunately, like a text of Scripture, it may mean one thing or another in the several minds using it.

XXI.

FAITH'S DISCIPLINE.

"What I do thou knowest not now; but thou shalt know hereafter." — JOHN xiii. 7.

> "And of the multitude,
> No man but in his hand
>   Holds some great gift misunderstood,
>   Some treasure for whose use or good
> His ignorance sees no demand."

YOUR wisdom is to renew and redouble your endeavor just to obey the commands of Jesus and make no clamor for comfort.

As to Christ's letting you go, you should not say or think it; it is so unjust to Him. He will never let you go, while you desire Him to keep you. You are one of His sheep; of whom He says, "My sheep hear my voice, and I know them, and they follow me; and I give unto them eternal life; and they shall never perish, neither shall any man pluck them out of my hand. My Father which gave them me, is greater than all; and no man is able to pluck them out of my Father's hand." I have no doubt that you dwell a great deal more on your unworthiness, than on His generosity. How dare you do that? If He chooses to magnify His grace to the unworthy, who are you that you should presume to exalt your ill-desert above His grace?

"You cannot see that you search for Him with all your heart."

Doubtless; but there are many other things which you cannot see: yet, being outside of them, you can believe. In this case you have too large an interest in the result to be admitted as a witness. You cite "inability to pray," it being, remember, the month of April. Well if you have been able to pray through the winter, you have been favored above many. If you could have looked into my parlor this morning at half-past six o'clock; into my heart, I was going to say, but I might as well say, into my slipper, you would have seen a form of godliness without the power. I was trying to pray, but an ape looks more like a man, than my endeavor looked like prayer. It was an utter failure. I was willing to think that something of it might be imputed to a chest utterly weakened by a cold. I shook myself; I walked up and down the room; there was nothing else I desired to do but praise and pray. But praise and pray I could not; for I had no more command of my brains than I had of Sherman's soldiers. Now this, which with me is an occasional experience, albeit it sometimes lasts from three to six weeks, and which, in its effects is much like a state of suspended animation, arising from the change from cold to heat, may with you be the more permanent result of a highly nervous temperament.

I do not mean fidgetty nervousness. I enter warmly into your strong expressions, for I have often said within myself, There never was such an utter imbecile and wreck of a man as I am! A breath of wind, or a degree of heat, is my master.

It is a good preparation for larger usefulness. Be not discouraged. Hope on. "At evening time it shall be light." It is plain to me that our Lord means to make something of you. I recognize His method. He is emptying your vessel in a way that appals you; but it is only that He may fill you with all the fullness of the blessed God. I have wondered over the masses of professors of religion, as you do, and wondered how they managed to go round and round, like the horse in the mill, for twenty, thirty, fifty years, some of them, apparently with no aspiration for enlargement.

There is faith in being troubled. If you had none, you too might be unconcerned. Now do not be cheated by Satan, as our first mother was. He will, very likely, be asking you, "Well, what have you gained by all your endeavors to wake up and be in earnest? Why not sleep on and be content as others are? What good have all these aspirations of yours done you?" Tell him for answer "Get thee behind me, Satan."

One explanation of your experiences is, perhaps, that God may discipline me through you. I am obliged to own myself at my wit's end. I cannot answer all questions. I cannot answer yours. I am convicted of ignorance. I must go humbly and ask Jesus. But suppose you were a chained slave, would it not be right for you to hold a lamp for those whose limbs were free? Will you not use such freedom as you have?

I got back from New York on Monday night after a week of real rest, and my Bible class on Tuesday afternoon took the benefit of it, for thoughts and words came like water from a mountain spring. But I took a little cold that same afternoon, and since then all the rest in New York goes for nothing. I tell you this because it reminds me that you "do not permit yourself to rest because you do not feel thus and so." Now I apprehend He requires you to rest unconditionally in Him; that is, without insisting that you must first feel thus or so. I am aware of how you will naturally reason about this. You will begin with saying, Surely, I ought to be more in earnest. I ought to be able to see that I search for Him with all my heart. I ought to find freedom and even delight in prayer. As long as you go on in this way,—I say it diffidently, for I am not sure that I am meeting your need,—it seems to me that you will perhaps, unconsciously, be seeking a righteousness in yourself, before you will fully accept the grace offered. But suppose, seeing you find nothing satisfactory in yourself, you just turn to our Father and ask Him to find all in Jesus; and to accept you for His sake; to take you just as you are, and make you what He wishes you to be. If you tell me, "Why, I have done that a thousand times;" then I say, Nevertheless, the knot in your problem is somewhere hereabouts. In your endeavors absolutely to give yourself to Jesus, you have somehow failed to give Him your trust. The misapprehension about feeling I look upon as almost universal; that is, there is a preconceived idea of a successful act of faith, involving very peculiar, if not overwhelming emotion; and a persuasion that if this be not realized, nothing is accomplished. Now the truth of the matter is, men catch sight of Jesus from every possible angle of vision, according to their endless varieties of need, seeing Him as just the Saviour needed for their own particular exigency; and the kind and degrees of emotion are as various as the peculiarities of circumstances. And so it follows that almost every preconceived idea is wholly unlike the actual experience. I suggest that for one week you endeavor, as far as possible, to repudiate and exclude all thoughts of yourself, and devote yourself to thoughts of your Lord. You would have to take some pains to provide your occupation. Give a day to the contemplation of Him as Creator; taking the first chapter of Genesis, first chapter of Colossians, and first chapter of Hebrews as your guide, and fourteen verses of the first chapter of John. The next day might be given to His justice, Rev. xv. 3. Another to His mercy, Ps. ciii. 13–18. Another to His self-sacrifice, Is. liii.; John iii. 16. Evidently a week spent in this way, with the intelligent design of subordinating self to Christ, would, with the blessing of the Holy Spirit, make a deep and lasting impression.

XXII.

FRUSTRATING GRACE.

"I do not frustrate the grace of God."—GAL. ii. 21.

"His wisdom ever waketh,
 His sight is never dim:
He knows the way He taketh,
 And I will walk with Him."

"And if there be a weight upon my breast
 Some vague impression of the day foregone,
Scarce knowing what it is, I fly to Thee
 And lay it down."

WITH the desire to comfort you, I told you yesterday that as you felt, so I felt; that I had no brains, and could not pray. It was a physical impossibility. With the same desire and design I want now to tell you that God having brought warm weather out of the South, to-night my hindrance is all gone, and I can pray. In this instance you see it was a matter of degrees of temperature. The same weather which merely thaws me out, may be wilting you. Nevertheless, hope thou in God, for he is the health of thy countenance and thy God, and you shall yet praise Him for all His manner of dealing with you. All this forenoon my thoughts were following your questions, and seeing, as I thought, a line of light running through them. But all the while I was being "driven up and down in the Adria" of business; and fearing just what has come upon me, namely, that when the leisure came, the thoughts would all be gone. So they are; and that is one of my keenest trials; the more interesting has to give way to the inexorable. But no; here is one of the thoughts given back to me; not a new thought, but one of vital moment; it is that no small part of your disappointment and sorrow arises from your meddling with the past and the future. Practically you are ever denying that the blood of Jesus cleanseth. For substance you are ever reasoning thus: "Yes, oh yes, in the abstract, and for others, I see that it is all true. But here is the peculiarity in my case, that I do thus and so, and therefore cannot expect the Lord to favor me." And thus you frustrate the grace of God; you make His promises of non-effect through your philosophy. You must give up all that. Nothing is of force to neutralize His word. The blood of Christ can and does wash away your sins. That is settled. Then, after having confessed the past, and received His forgiveness, you have no right to dishonor Him by reviving the past, as though His blood had not sufficient adequacy. As to the future, it is written, "My God shall supply all your need." He will love and keep you to the end, and you have nothing at all to do with the future. If you commit your way unto Him now, the promise is, that He will bring it to pass, "What time I am afraid, I will trust in the Lord." Can you possibly find a better example? If your fears come upon you, run to Him. He is a high rock, a strong tower, a sure defense, and refuge. It is Satan that drives you first to the past, and then to the future. There is no resting-place in the one or in the other. But in the Lord Jehovah there is everlasting strength, present strength. Renew your self-consecration to him as often as you are disquieted. That is just putting yourself and all your disquiets into His hands — precisely what He wishes, invites, commands you to do.

Thank you for "Little Ballard's Praying and Resignation." I am not ashamed to own to you that it brought the tears into my eyes, to the serious hindrance of my reading. I know nothing more beautiful than these illustrations of faith in children. I know an instance, equally beautiful, of the son of my friends, Mr. and Mrs. M. He had set his heart on going to his aunt in Wisconsin. His mother repeatedly replied to his entreaties, "It is impossible; the season is advanced, and I know of no one going out, by whom I could send you." At last she said, "Go and tell Jesus your desire. If He wishes you to go, He will open the way." The little fellow took her at her word, and pressed his suit, and Jesus opened the way, and he went to Wisconsin. This is but a meagre outline of the facts. Once Mrs. M. would have been backward to give such counsel to her son. Once she rebelled against the will of God, when He took an infant. Now she takes everything from Him lovingly, walking through all sorts of trials serenely, stayed on Him. Your "dim idea of such a life of purest joy" is not in the least dim to my eye. Most undoubtedly you are right in your conjecture that Jesus painted that ideal in your soul, both to raise your desire and stimulate your endeavors for it. In my judgment, you are not far from it now. You think "you do not aim at being a devoted Christian." Doubtless he who attains most of such devotion to Christ is least able to esteem himself the Christian he ought to be, because the attainment must always light the way to something beyond, which ought to be attained. So St. Paul testifies, Phil. iii. 13. Assuredly "our views of consecration do expand as we advance." It is most reasonable to long to be able to say, "My Beloved is mine." Persist, and you will assuredly succeed; nay, you are succeeding day by day, and presently your eyes will be opened, as were the eyes of Elisha's servant at Dothan. Become simply natural; like a little child, if you can; for I confess to you, I sometimes find it a very difficult attainment. I had a lesson as I was walking over to C. on Sunday night, anxious as to whether I could possibly say anything to benefit the children.

"What right have you to be anxious?"

I answered, "None, Lord;" and gave it up.

It was He who put the question, and He answered His own question.

Doubtless the reason "you do not thank Him for the Atonement," "His Word," "Himself," is that the object is too large, too multiform. You do thank Him for the gleams of light and love from each, as you are enabled to catch them. Be thankful that you are prompted and enabled to do that. Taste one verse at a time, and thank Him for it. Ask the Comforter to enable you to get the utmost profit out of it.

XXIII.

GOD'S PART AND OURS.

"For it is God which worketh in you both to will and to do of His good pleasure." — PHIL. ii. 13.

"The look, the fashion of God's ways
Love's life-long study are;
She can be bold, and guess, and act,
When reason would not dare."

I DO not wonder that you sometimes get confused betwixt the Lord's part of the work, and your own. If Methusaleh was a thinking man, I would give something to know how far he had thought up on that subject in his nine hundred and sixty-ninth year. Apropos of God's providence in providing boarding-places in the summer, in the country, a minister's wife said to me yesterday, "I believe you think the Lord has always found one for you, but I think He has left us to shift for ourselves." I replied, "Now why do you say that? Why not believe in Him at least as much as you believe in me?"

"Because I don't see Him."

"But I should be sorry to think that you trust me only when you see me."

"Ah, but that seems different."

I might have told her, had it been quite modest, "I always ask the Lord to send me where I can do most good; but, on your own acknowledgment, you don't do that. How then can you expect Him to take special care of you?"

Yet I am by no means without my problems. For example, I had predetermined to push certain business matters to-day, to the advantage of my purse. But I found that an article written for the "Recorder" was arrested when half set up because some statements needed qualifying. In my wisdom, or folly, I decided that that article must be put through, in season for the occasion for which it was written, as being of more account to Christ and His cause than the money. Now no business man would justify me in this. I don't feel sure that our Lord Himself looks upon me as justified in it. Sometimes I am pulled in pieces between the desire to do all possible good, and the desire so to perform life's work-a-day business that none may have right to charge that I am less than true to myself and family in that. If there are disciples of Christ who have no experience of this perplexity, I do not envy, but pity them.

About your friend who says foolish things, and excites your wonder, why she is left to do so; I can see a way through that. One of the most valuable attainments we ever make is humble penitence. What teaches this so effectually as our own blunders? What if our Lord means that she shall sink low in her own esteem, through the discovery of her folly? In one way I shall dissent from brother G.'s way of putting it: I don't believe "the Lord expected she would behave herself with propriety." He knew she would not. But may He not have purposed to overrule that impropriety to bring her into right relations to Himself? What would become of us were we cast off every time we err? Oh the long-suffering kindness of our Lord! Mr. G. is right; the Lord does require us to behave well. And yet, again, it is just as true, that we do so only as He works in us to will and to do of His good pleasure. You say "you want to be known as a Christian without effort," that is as a spontaneous Christian. Well, keep on desiring. "Blessed are they that hunger and thirst, for they shall be filled."

You are hearing much of the labors of Mr. Moody of Chicago. Let me tell you something of him. His history may well encourage you to hope in the Lord, and in His unstinted grace. In utter disregard of the judgment of his friends he left his home, a benighted town in western Massachusetts and came to Boston. He was unconscious of dependence upon God. Two weeks' vain pursuit of a situation, humbled his pride of self-sufficiency to the extent of willingness to speak with his uncle, a pious man, who knew how to be silent, and when to speak.

Said Moody, "I have wasted two weeks here to no purpose, and now I'm going to New York to seek an opening."

"Yes," replied his uncle, "and there you will waste more weeks; for here there is some one, if asked, to speak for you, there, not one."

Well, I can't do anything here; I've tried in vain."

"You have not yet asked me."

"Have you got any vacancy?"

"That depends upon circumstances. I have a position I could give you. But I will not give it to you except upon your agreement to comply with my conditions; one of which is this: that you shall go regularly to Mount Vernon Church, and into the Sabbath-school."

The consent was given, and Moody himself told me this: "My young companion took me to a seat in the gallery. When the sermon began I fell asleep. My companion jogged me and pointed to the minister. I endeavored to listen for a little, and fell asleep again. Again my companion aroused me. This time I kept awake, and listened." He went also into the Sabbath-school; but was mortified in the discovery of the superior acquaintance with the Bible of persons considerably younger than himself. His teacher, who was at that time in my employ, told me that the first perceptible awakening of M.'s intellect came when the class were studying the career of Moses. He suddenly looked up and said: "This Moses, I suppose, was what you'd call a smart man, wasn't he?" He was carefully and faithfully followed up by his teacher. After a time he presented himself to the church committee, expressing his desire to join the church. Ten of us, with the most kindly interest and good wishes for this new-comer, and with all the intelligence we were able to bring to bear upon him, failed to elicit any satisfactory evidence that he even knew what was regeneration. He could not say he thought Christ had done anything for himself. Apparently he knew no more of Jesus than did Festus when he informed Agrippa that the accusers of Paul had certain questions against him of their own superstition, and of one Jesus who was dead, whom Paul affirmed to be alive. It might indeed be doubted, whether Moody held with Festus, or with Paul. The committee judged it wise to wait till M. obtained some intelligent apprehension of the Lord. Meanwhile several members of the committee, concurring with his teacher, invited him to their homes, and like Aquila and Priscilla, expounded unto him the way of God more perfectly.

This delaying of his admission for six months, or more, Moody himself assured me, "was the best thing we ever did." No doubt in God's hands it contributed to that freedom from self-conplacency which now so endears this dear brother to all who desire and pray for his largest usefulness. He remained with us only about two years. No doubt he was gathering all the while materials for future use. But God's gracious intent to make him a chosen vessel, did not reveal itself till he had removed to Chicago. There the Lord met him in the way, and anointed him for His work. If you ask, Why thus anoint him and not me? I can answer only, Even so, Lord, for so it seemed good to Thee. Walking the streets of that city, surveying the pit falls for the unwary, and the fearful sluiceways to perdition through the innumerable saloons, drinking, gambling, dancing, etc., the Spirit of God came mightily upon him. Meeting a stranger, he impetuously demanded of him, What can we do for Chicago? The stranger, he told me, stared, as one saying within himself, "A crazy man, no doubt!" Nothing daunted, he hired a pew in church, and then a second, and filled these with recruits rescued from saloons. "But I found," he said, that I was filling a vessel with holes; they did not look after my men. Then I hired a small room and taught them myself, then a larger and a larger room, till I had one of the largest saloons in Chicago." Thus he came to hear his call to drop secular business, and devote his life to saving souls. Two youth, sons of a distinguished lawyer, cleaved to him, spite of their father's positive prohibition. The father knew of Jesus perhaps as much as did Festus, and cared as little. But this influence of Mr. Moody on his sons was an enigma he was curious to look into. He posted off to search for, and found Mr. M.

"My boys, Mr. Moody, have caused me many anxious hours; but though I have known them all their days, you have acquired more influence over them in six weeks than I have ever had. I don't understand it. I want to know about it."

"Oh," said Mr. M., "that's very simple! It's only the love of Jesus; do you know anything of that?"

"No; he must confess he did not."

"Well, you must come to my meetings, and I will tell you."

"But I'm driven with work, and don't know when and where they are."

"Never mind; next meeting I'll send the boys to show you the way." And he came, and came again.

Since then Mr. M.'s history has been pretty well and widely known. He lives by faith on the Son of God; and like a child in his Father's house. Aye, and Christ lives in him. I thank the dear Lord that M. and I have long been friends. I am specially indebted to the Master and to brother M. that he has more than once put me up to work I might not else have thought to do. One day describing a certain case to him, I read the letter I had written to meet it. He exclaimed, "I must have that. Promise me you'll make a tract of it." And so I did. "Seeing Jesus." Again, passing one day, through Scollay Square, oppressed with the sense of my inefficiency, and no less with my incompetency, some one slipped his arm through mine, and looking up I found brother M. "I've got some work for you," he said. "Alas, I was bemoaning myself that there was no work in me." So then at his request and for a particular use I wrote "A Word to the Sorrowing."

Shall I express sorrow that you have been ill, when our beloved Jesus sent the illness? I was not sorry myself when I was so ill that my physician came three times a day for a week, and did not expect me to live. I think it is good to live, because there is work, loving work to do for our Lord and for His lambs. But I am not in love with life. Nor yet am I so spiritual, to-day at any rate, as to be fit to comment on 2 Cor. v. 8. I suspect that the want of physical stamina more than anything else makes me at times long for the end. I do abhor sin; and do feel that it must be ineffably blessed to have done with it forever. But I cannot quite find the Apostle's declaration true for me, that "whilst we are at home in the body we are absent from the Lord." Does he not say to the Ephesians, "Ye are no more strangers and foreigners, but fellow-citizens with the saints, and of the household of God, an habitation of God through the Spirit"? I am not sure that he may not have meant something which I can respond to. If he meant to say, as he does elsewhere say, that "we are strangers," all true Christians, and that those who make themselves at home in the body, are absent from the Lord, I could assent to that, easily. But I am not at home in the body. I feel myself only a lodger for a night, and nothing keeps me from singing perpetually,

> "To Jesus, the crown of my life
> My soul is in haste to be gone,"

but the obvious disloyalty of preferring my comfort to His will and work. Beyond a question it must be far better to be with Jesus in sinless holiness, and so in perfect oneness; for that is the very blessedness of heaven. But I have not finished the work He has given me to do. I have not learned the lessons, nor acquired the virtues He placed me here to acquire. Nor can I possibly believe it to be better to depart and be with Christ, till this is done. I know it is a common thought that more can be learned in heaven in an hour, than on earth in a year; but I am firm in the conviction that such common thoughts, as commonly understood, are without a shadow of warrant. God has declared that all things work together for good to them that love Him. Among these "all things," our detention on the earth is most surely to be reckoned. The skillful cultivator transplants his shrubs and trees in their best season; of which he alone can be the judge. So, and much more, our Lord alone can know the best season for our transplanting. Therefore I would not dare be "in haste to be gone." Possibly the Apostle's meaning was, that the presence of Jesus, or to be with Jesus, is in itself, or absolutely, far better than any condition known to us this side of that heavenly presence. It appears to me that that may be quite true, and yet not involve any such inference as that it would be far better, to-day, for me or for you to depart and be with Christ. Beyond a question, from the hour of our receiving the Holy Ghost He dwells with us and in us; charging Himself with our education, leading us step by step to the acquisition of each lesson provided for us in the Divine programme; and then we graduate on earth, and are admitted to a higher and celestial school. According to the Bible figure, we are " gathered as a shock of corn fully ripe, to the garner of the Lord."

XXIV.

PERPLEXITIES.

"Call upon me in the day of trouble: I will deliver thee, and thou shalt glorify me."— Ps. l. 15.

" There are in this loud stunning tide
  Of human care and crime,
With whom the melodies abide
  Of the everlasting chime;
Who carry music in their heart
  Through dusky lane and wrangling mart
Plying their daily toil with busier feet,
Because their secret souls a holy strain repeat."

" O eyes that are weary, and hearts that are sore!
Look off unto Jesus; now sorrow no more!"

COMING into town this morning, I fell to thinking upon the perplexities our Lord God sends us all. And His good Spirit the Comforter, comforted me with some thoughts I wish to share with you. Doubtless the cry, "Why am I thus?" sooner or later comes up out of the suffering experience of every child of God. For twenty-five years, with intervals long or short, of peace and quietness, I have had these experiences of extreme perplexity, and consciousness of being at my very wits' end, and void of all wisdom to meet the demands of a seeming emergency and crisis. The emergencies of twenty-five years, as you see, have not only come, but also gone, and leave me unscathed. While impending they have often seemed fateful as destiny. They were but our Heavenly Father's helps to a clearer vision of Jesus, and to more perfect sympathy with Him. In His hands they have proved nothing but blessings. And I am able to testify for Him who said, "Seek first the kingdom of God and His righteousness, and all these things shall be added unto you," that His word is true. So have I done; and so have I found. But this morning the thought was: God's method with me is not to be judged or estimated by any visible or known adaptation to a particular good result; but to be accepted as His; and as the most advantageous, simply because it is His; and because that which it secures will surely be the best and most desirable, and must needs be. I am at no loss to conjecture how this may be. I can easily believe, first, that my Lord desires to bring me into the most perfect sympathy and oneness with Him. Second, that this consists peculiarly (1) in a profound and unalterable deference to the Father's will; (2) in great tenderness of sensibility towards the burden-bearing, and the suffering. And, third, that He would bring me into the exercise of a faith in Him that nothing can disturb. But to know whether a tree, or a Christian faith, can be uprooted, or blown down, it is needful that it should be blown upon, most furiously, by every wind of heaven. If it stands bravely through it all, we have an evident and most encouraging result, not to be made evident and encouraging in any other way.

Let us bring this close home to our souls. You and I have problems which as yet we are unable to solve. We are held in suspense. We can wait; looking up and saying, and feeling too, Dearest Lord, I thank Thee for this suspense. It throws me more directly, frequently, constantly on Thee. It bids me cry out of the depths of my heart, "My soul, wait thou only upon God; for my expectation is from Him. He only is my rock and my salvation." In John xvii. 20, 21, Jesus prays for us, that we all may be one, "as Thou, Father, art in me, and I in Thee; that they also may be one in us." And in John xv. 9, He says, "As the Father hath loved me, so have I loved you." Now I am going to believe that, just because Jesus said it. And believing that, I may well rest, firm as the everlasting hills, upon His love; believing that if anywhere among all the inexhaustible treasures of my Lord, there were a single thing better for me than the things which try me most, then I should have it. Now I feel the better for telling you this, which I know is true; and I hope we both shall be the stronger to endure, all the days of our appointed time, till our change come. When an almost irrepressible longing to go comes upon me, I cannot but demand of myself, How dare you, seeing God has given you so many precious souls who are comforted by you with the very comfort wherewith you yourself are comforted of God? And so I appeal to Him, to strengthen me to hold on, and hold out, to the end; striving to hold to other lips the cup of consolation He hands me for them.

How blessed it is to be a minister and an apostle of Jesus Christ! Blessed that we are such, you and I; albeit innocent of the laying on of human hands! Paul said to the Corinthian Christians, "Ye see your calling, brethren." Alas, it is to be feared that many Christians do not see it! To be called of God, and sent by Jesus Christ, were it only to a single soul, is something infinitely superior to being ordained of men. Would to God that all ordained ministers were thus conscious of their heavenly calling. Such consciousness would deliver them from a thousand ignoble anxieties, jealousies, and evil-surmisings. Upon careful reading of some of the articles in "The Witness," it seems to me that I find ground for fear that some of its writers are inclined to press their favorite idea beyond its proper limits. Thus, for example, it is quite true that we find persons in circumstances which make it proper to say to them, According to my apprehension of your position, the one thing required of you, is to believe that a full, present salvation is offered to you by our Lord Jesus, and that you should now accept both it and Him. Meanwhile it is just as true of other persons that their circumstances call for a different communication. While the former class are intensely concerned to see Jesus, and their minds are fully set on forsaking all for Him, the latter are comparatively careless of finding Him, and by no means resolved on making any considerable sacrifice for Him. And I think our Lord has made it no inconsiderable part of our duty, to search out the actual condition of these different classes, and with much prayer and painstaking, to prescribe their appropriate course to each. Can we escape the conviction that the larger part of professing Christians do not even propose to be candidates for the highest joys, so freely offered? Alas, I have found more than one or two, who have declined joys conditioned upon self-denying and persistent service!

You ask, How can one who is more conscious of hunger, and thirst, and need, than of anything else, praise God as one of His children can who can adopt the couplet,

> "With every longing satisfied,
> And full salvation blessed."

Why, my dear friend, praise Him for that hunger and thirst. It is one of God's best gifts. Jesus declares it blessed. It is the sure precursor of being filled with all the fullness of the blessed God. "Must you wait until you reach 'love's own country,' before you can drink such refreshing draughts from 'The deep sweet well of love?'" No, indeed! For our Immanuel says, "Ho, every one that thirsteth, come ye to the waters, and he that hath no money; come ye, buy and eat; yea, come, buy wine and milk without money and without price." When President Edwards was exercised with the same longing to be filled with Jesus, he resolved to do all in his power to encourage, increase, and intensify the longing. Doubtless that is just what our Lord would have you do. Jesus is "the rose of Sharon; the lily of the valleys; the chiefest among ten thousand; the one altogether lovely." "His name is as ointment poured forth." The more you cherish Him, the more you will find Him so. You ask, "Will He always deal thus with me?" Meaning, I presume, "Will He always hide Himself from me?" "Must I wait till I wear my crown, before I taste the sweetness of His love?"

I answer, Every hour He seems to keep you waiting, He is but detaching you from everything that holds you back. His arms are wide extended. You may come into them this moment; and actually do come into His arms to the extent of your desire. There is a more perfect union for which you are longing, and towards which you are tending. There is no holding back on His part; but your eyes are in part holden. You do but see men as trees walking. This very moment you may, unchecked, lay your head upon His bosom, and there rest forever. It is what He would have you do. Long delay to do this, has infused distrust; has made you timid; has led you to reason endlessly, "If I were only thus or so; if I had only done this or that; then might I cast myself on Him, and take my fill of love divine." You are free to come just as you are; but so long as you doubt, you will not come. The moment will come, you are pressing earnestly towards it, when you will let go the last doubt, and rest on Him.[1] The time draws near. When it comes, it will be the gift of God. You will know it to be so, and, "Or ever you are aware, your soul will make you like the chariots of Amminadib." Canticles vi. 12. You will be borne along through "love's own country," in the bosom of the Lord of the country, with fullness of joy, as on the wings of the wind. "Will Jesus be tired of you?" What, He who says, "Thou shall love the Lord thy God with all thy heart, soul, mind, and strength?" Who says also, "If a man love me, he will keep my words; and my Father will love him, and we will come unto him and make our abode with Him." Do you think He will? Would you be tired of one who in like manner was seeking to deserve your love? "Why can't you revel in the ocean of His love?" Only believe His own assertion, "Underneath are the everlasting arms," and nothing can prevent your doing so. Were you ever so advanced a Christian, so long as you remain in the body hunger and thirst must needs at once attest your sonship, and that absence from

[1] See the fulfillment of this in her own letter, page 247.

your Lord, which constrained Paul to say that "to depart and be with Christ is far better." Why, I have prayed for years, with an intensity of entreaty words cannot convey: Lord, I beseech Thee, I entreat Thee, I implore Thee, I conjure and adjure Thee, by all the love Thou bearest to Thine own dear Son, that Thou make me as holy as it is possible for Almighty God to make me for His dear sake. Often I add, as soon as Thou canst for Christ's dear sake. And He is doing it. I say it not from anything I see, but because He is as good as His word, and I cannot doubt Him. A vision of faith's coming victory is a perpetual light in my soul. I cannot discern its form; but its inspiration is none the less for that. It is a sure word of prophecy. He has done and is doing great things for me, whereof I am glad. What He is doing for me, He is also doing for thee, beloved.

XXV.

REALIZING JESUS.

The disciple whom Jesus loved said unto Peter, It is the Lord." — JOHN xxi. 7.

"O my sweet Jesus! hear the sighs
Which unto Thee I send;
To Thee my inmost spirit cries —
My being's hope and end."

YOU do "realize Jesus." Have you a shadow of a doubt that Jesus is? When you open at John xiii. 1, and read, "He loved them unto the end," have you the shadow of a doubt that He loves His disciples to-day, as truly as then? Do you doubt that Jesus speaks to each of us in John xiv., xv., and xvi.? Do you doubt that in John xvii. 24, He included you and me? When you read the healing of the man thirty-eight years at the pool; or of the raising of the young ruler's daughter; or of Lazarus, have you any difficulty in realizing Jesus? Do you not so realize Him as to feel, "Yes, that is just like Him; just what I should expect of Him; just what I should feel sure He would do in such circumstances?" Can you not feel usually how He would decide or act under such and such circumstances? Certainly you can and do; and in that lies the evidence that you realize Jesus. I anticipate your saying, "But what I mean is, I want to realize just how He feels towards me." Well, He feels just as He told you He would in John xiv. 23, xv. 9, and xvii. 24; Jer. xxxi. 3. He loves you, and He loves you so tenderly that He cannot stay away from you; He dwells in your very heart. "But I cannot realize that," you answer. In other words, you cannot believe Him. Why can't you believe Him? "Oh, I can't believe that Jesus can love and dwell with so sinful a being as I am." He knew when He adopted you, as He knew of Peter, James, and John, that you were and would be sinful; but He also knew that you would be a penitent sinner; therefore He finds even your sinfulness no bar to the fulfillment of His word. "But you want a more impressing conviction of His love." "And," you add, "if He is more ready to give than I to receive, why does He not give it then?" I do not know. "Even so, Father, for so it seemeth good in Thy sight." That is to say, I don't know why He does not give you the realization of His compliance with His promise; that He does actually give all He promises, I am not able to doubt. You remember His answer to some who made requests of Him: "According to your faith be it unto you." It seems inevitable to conclude, that that which you desire of Him, hinges upon the exercise of a confidence in Him which He expects of you, and for which you are accountable. That would seem to imply that you can trust Him; that a foundation for that trust is laid in His promise. The promise is His; you know it to be His; you know Him to be faithful, and that He cannot forfeit His word; therefore you can, ought, must, lovingly trust in Him, when He says, "Whosoever cometh unto me, I will in no wise cast out." Be sure of this; there is no backwardness on His part. Somehow your willingness and ability to receive does not keep pace with His willingness and desire to give.

I am sorry, dear friend, even "to seem hard upon you," but it is not I that am hard. I say to you, only what I am compelled a thousand times to say to myself, "O thou of little faith!" It is true, my small faith never staggers at the personal presence and ceaseless love and helpfulness of Jesus; nevertheless, I am sometimes inexpressibly tired of the conflict of life. Not that I would abridge my term of service a day, or an hour; but I do not handle the problems of life with the wisdom which I am persuaded stronger faith would supply; and I find abundant reason for the belief that multitudes are turning life's opportunities and privileges to better account. So you see that this brother of yours, like yourself, is not backward in finding hindrances to perfect peace. Well, when I am thus troubled, I go to my Lord, just as I am; go instantly; go believingly; but I often have to wait for the feeling I would like to have. Suppose you could at any moment work yourself up to the ecstatic consciousness you so much desire; would its possession contribute as much to your faith, as when given at His own sovereign good will and time? You see I am trying to go all round this subject; it is all I can do; to drop a hint here and there, and leave it for the good Comforter to combine and harmonize the hints, if He please. I do not say that you might have exactly what your soul cries out for; that I presume to be an immediate sensation — I do not mean it offensively — but that word comes nearest to my idea; and sensation or sensuous impression, is what multitudes do get here and there, under pressure and excitement, and miscall it faith. But the thing I must say, is, that you may instantly, actually, thoroughly give yourself to Jesus; and He will instantly, actually, thoroughly receive you. This I have no doubt you have done, as far as you comprehend your privilege. You do not recognize the compass and significance of one of your own decisions. I dare say you sometimes talk with yourself to this effect: "Yes, true, I did tell the Lord at such a time, Lord I give myself to Thee; but it did n't amount to much, mere words; I did n't see that anything came of it."

Now just there I challenge you. I deny your right to hold such language even to yourself. It is the language of unbelief. Can you deny that you did then and there mean to give yourself to Jesus? And dare you deny that He received what you tendered? Will you accuse Him of insincerity and unfaithfulness? "Oh no! that is the last thing you would wish to do. But how are you going to escape the imputation of having done just that? I presume I know; you will fall back on that miserable old refuge which has the power to take the soul out of all language: "I could n't seem to think that what I said amounted to anything or that it effected anything." Is n't that doing great unjustice alike to language and to yourself? Language used with honest intent does mean something; does accomplish something. If you give yourself to Jesus in honest meaning words, you actually give yourself. Why, every-day life is full of such doings, and who doubts their significance? A man stands up in the church and says, "I avouch the Lord Jehovah to be my God." His words are full of meaning; everybody recognizes their meaning and holds him henceforth to have adopted the service of Christ. A woman stands up in church or parlor and says, "I take this man to be my husband." We do indeed sometimes say, " It does not seem as if that brief ceremony could effect such a total change in the lives of two persons;" but we never doubt the reality of what is effected by the avowal. We know that a simple yes or no, ratifies a bargain of vast importance between one merchant and another. Only a word! True, only a word, but right words, how significant! Allow their significance, and it does seem to me, that you might come at once into soul satisfying realization of your relation to Jesus.

After all, I am not wise; I am only a child, a very little child. I often tell our Lord so. I say to Him, Dear Master, Thou knowest my ignorance. And again, "O God, thou knowest my foolishness; and my sin is not hid from Thee." Psalm lxix. 5. One day one truth seems clear to me as the noonday sun. Another day some other truth shines so brightly as to leave all other truths for the moment in the dim distance. Very possibly you have expected too much from me, because of having found some part of my testimony to your purpose. Our Lord means you shall "cease from man whose breath is in his nostrils," and get your supplies from Himself. True, He does use man intermediately; but also true it is, that sometimes He chooses to be His own interpreter, and to take His own time for it. He has also a choice, and a reason for His choice of messengers. I am inclined to suspect that the word which will set you free will be intrusted to some messenger other than myself. You know that your sanctification is God's purpose and intent; that He has undertaken it, and is carrying it on. "Not in a way satisfactory to me," you may say, "for if I were only convinced that this is actually advancing, and in the best manner, I could be reconciled to anything." Perhaps not; I am firmly convinced that God's method with me is the very best; I would not have it altered; and yet I find it as little to my taste as being flayed alive. I can and do often ask Him, not to spare the rod for the child's crying; but it is a rod still, and I don't like it. The best I can say is, "I will do my best, dear Lord, to endure for Thy sake." Often and often am I ready to exclaim, "My soul chooseth strangling and death, rather than my life." And yet, have I anything to complain of? Nothing! And do I wish to go? No, indeed! not till I have finished the work He has given me to do; learned the lessons He gives me to learn; borne the burdens He has chosen me to bear; and "filled up that which is behind of the afflictions of Christ in my flesh for His body's sake." A Christian lady said to me yesterday, "I understand why these troubles are upon me; it is because of my self-will. It has got to be subdued." It is worth a good deal to understand the why. Perhaps the why you are thus, is, that you do not read His Word with that simplicity which takes each utterance as from Him to thee. Perhaps you do not enough use the intelligence He has given you to search out the characteristics of Him who thus speaks to you, as they are imbedded in what He says.

That much remains that is unsatisfactory to you, is no more true of you than of me. For, though I can say unhesitatingly, "I am my Beloved's, and my Beloved is mine;" "There is now no condemnation, ... for the law of the spirit of life in

Christ Jesus hath set me free from the law of sin and death;" still I count not myself to have attained anything, — not that I deny any attainments really made, but because I am so necessarily and overwhelmingly conscious of the unattained, that I forget the things behind, in my longing desire for those which remain to be struggled for. Hope thou in God; and praise for what you have received. Do not think it modest to ignore that.

XXVI.

COMPLETENESS IN JESUS.

"Know ye not that your body is the temple of the Holy Ghost which is in you?" — 1 Cor. vi. 19.

> With hearts so vile how dare we venture,
>   Holy Ghost! to love Thee so?
> And how canst thou, with such compassion,
>   Bear so long with things so low?
> Holy Ghost! possess Thy children
>   Give us grace, and keep us Thine;
> Thy tender fires within us kindle,
>   Blessed Spirit! Dove Divine!"

THE Bible class lesson this morning was Colossians ii. 10: "And ye are complete in Him." It has such a precious lesson for you that I must send it to you. Your disappointment in respect to your own progress will be alleviated by it. Each Christian is a temple of the Holy Ghost. You are such a temple; not yet finished, but being advanced day by day by Him who formed you for Himself.

On Berkeley Street a new church is being built, on land reclaimed from the river. Nearly a year ago they were driving piles whereon to lay the foundation. When we went into the country, in June, I said to myself, we shall see great progress when we return. But when I went down to see it, they had not reached even the top of the doors. Shapeless blocks and bits of stone were lying around, and the workmen were not idle, but the work is large, and to be built for long continuance. Meanwhile this slowly advancing edifice is all complete in the mind of the architect. It is completely illustrated in his drawings, some of which I have seen. If the workmen live, if disasters do not overtake them, if the blessing of God shall favor, by and by the building will be complete to the eye of every beholder. Now about yourself, there is no if but one. "You shall know, if you follow on to know the Lord," for his own mouth hath spoken it. "Blessed is the man that endureth temptation"— that is — the discipline of life : "for when he is tried, he shall receive the crown of life which the Lord hath promised to them that love Him." You are being tried, and it is your loving Lord who is trying you. He is tenderly desirous that you shall endure. He has prayed for thee that thy faith fail not. How prone you are to think, "Oh, my trials are only the natural consequences of my sinfulness, and of my many failures in duty," and so you think the blessing promised to the man that endureth temptation "can't be intended for you." But suppose now, that the last sin you committed was one of indolence, or of impulsiveness ; of covetousness, or of lavish extravagance ; it matters little which, or what. It is your Lord who permits a temptation to meet you on your accessible side. Temptation does not come on any other side. Then, do you not see that there is in the temptations coming under a natural law, or in the way of natural consequence, no bar whatever to the supposition of its being Divinely sent, and for your highest good? At present you are enduring the trial of hope deferred. You desire the immediate realization of Jesus' love for you. You believe the fact; but you cannot realize Jesus and his love in it. So far as your inability to do this is the effect of sin, your disappointment will surely intensify your abhorrence of sin. Is not that a great gain? Does any one love God and holiness, who does not equally hate sin and Satan? We are not so apt to think of this; but we must hate sin, as God hates it; and it does not appear that we can do this except as we learn its hatefulness from its disastrous influence upon our usefulness and happiness. What you want is absolutely sure and certain; namely, that our Lord should educate you for the everlasting enjoyment of his friendship and service. That He is doing. He says so: "Yea I have loved thee with an everlasting love; therefore with loving kindness have I drawn thee." "You are no more a stranger and foreigner, ... but built on the foundation of the apostles and prophets, Jesus Christ Himself being the chief corner-stone. In whom all the building fitly framed together groweth unto an holy temple in the Lord; in whom ye also are builded together for an habitation of God through the Spirit." For what has Jesus reconciled you to God? "To present you holy, unblamable, and unreprovable in His sight." But Christ is still preached to you; "that we may present you perfect in Christ Jesus." It is a progressive work. Some few Christians appear to be brought, by the grace of God, to a point from which it is but one step to that fullness of joy and peace in believing which you so much crave. God sends some Christian friend to indicate that one step, and it is seen and taken. Others protest they cannot see it. One dear and honored friend, himself a preacher and teacher of righteousness, to whom, more perhaps than to any other living preacher, I owe under God, my own great joy and peace, I watched attentively and lovingly for thirty years and more; during all which time he bemoaned himself as "a victim to the servile spirit," and unable to rise from it into the spirit of a son. There were not wanting those who for this pronounced — shall I say, flippant condemnation, of this man of God? But his Lord had assigned him a work among the problems of holy living and holy thinking, of which, the larger part even of teachers, know very little. Through these it was appointed him to work his way into the serene light. And, some years ago, in God's own best time, he was enabled to emerge from his hard fought contest, conqueror, and more than conqueror, through Him who loved him, and gave not only Himself for him, but also the Divine Comforter, to dwell with him and in him, and to guide him into all truth. On the same general principle I am confident our Lord is dealing with you. He will either presently give you the realization of Himself which you crave, or he will have a good and sufficient reason for reserving it. Either way, He will assuredly supply all you need through the riches of His grace in Christ Jesus.

XXVII.

LESSONS.

> " Over and over again,
>   No matter which way I turn
> I always find in the Book of Life
>   Some lesson I have to learn.
> I must take my turn at the mill,
>   I must grind out the golden grain,
> I must work at my task with a resolute will
>   Over and over again."

HOW evident is the hand of God in this transfer from E. to M.! While your minds were in a flutter of agitation, no result was reached, except the decision to do nothing. These cases of conscience in which our Lord for a season, and for His own wise purposes, withholds the light we crave, are most profitable. They compel heart-searching, and heart-purifying. Our dear Lord has been preparing you to go to M., "in the fullness of the blessing of the gospel of Christ." Seldom have I been more pressed in spirit to go on my way praying, than when in Chicago I started to find the friends whose hospitality I was to enjoy. I prayed most earnestly that I might go to them in the fullness of that blessing, and that I might be specially useful to some one of the household. I found a dear daughter who is going by the same way my dear May passed out of life. I found her very timid and reluctant to speak; less from want of will, I think, than from want of habit. I trust the Lord will follow our conversation with His blessing.

Tell J. "Whom the Lord loveth, He chasteneth." My saying so, wont do much for her; but her finding it so, will. I was thinking on my way to the office, what a wonderful thing is experience! Like a ticket to the Athenæum, it is "Not Transferable." We may mention what we have found true, but it does not become true to another until the Lord embodies it in the experience of that other. I have not a doubt that you will follow on. Yes, John x. 27, 28, is all your own. When I said there was but one if, I did not assert that there was one. I simply sought to strengthen you by the assurance that there was not another. I have found a sweet lesson in John xxi. 7 : "The disciple whom Jesus loved said, 'It is the Lord.'" The loved and loving disciple sees Jesus in every event, incident, and experience.

Sunday evening. — I have thought of you, and prayed for you, under the belief that this is your first Sabbath in M. The Lord make it a sure earnest of a most useful and blessed ministry both for you and for Mr. G. I am sure you have prayed, "If Thy presence go not with us, carry us not up hence." Nor have I any doubt that He, the Comforter, has gone with you. At our prayer-meeting this evening, the precious and instructive narrative of Cornelius the Centurion and Peter was read. How encouraging it is! The Lord lifts for us a veil, and shows us in one place an inquirer praying; in another place, miles and miles away, He shows a religious teacher praying. He sends the one to the other, and adds His blessing to the message carried. Peter went as soon as bidden. It does not appear that he troubled himself either about what he was to say, or how he was to say it. He went to preach Christ; he did preach Christ, in such words as were given him. "It was given him in that same hour what he should speak." This pledge is as good and sure for us, as it was for him. Is it not good to wait on the Spirit? I have done that from the first hour I believed; but I have often thought, had I my religious life to live over again, I would not be satisfied with my past measure of looking to Him. I would more than ever reverently and lovingly insist that He should give me my work day by day, hour by hour. Nothing I am sure would please Him more. It does seem that a vast amount of unproductive, and so discouraging, labor, might be avoided, just by getting always our direction from the Lord. We read that David inquired of the Lord, "Shall I go up against the Philistines?" "And the Lord answered, Go up, and I will deliver them into thy hands." We are ready to say, Now if I could only be directed like that, then I could work with a will; as though our guidance were any less certain or available because it is given in another way. "If thou canst believe," said Jesus, "all things are possible to him that believeth." It is only to trust Him as the true and faithful Friend He says He is. When challenged to believe, many disciples cast about them for some precept or promise to fit some peculiarity of their condition, rather than turn the confidence of their hearts on Christ Himself. It is written, "Let thine heart keep my commandments." When once I take Jesus to my heart as the Lamb of God, the Good Shepherd, the Bread of Life, the Son of Consolation, the Unchanging Friend, then it is easy to accept any one of His promises as the sure earnest, aye, as the complete fulfillment of the thing promised. Nothing seems too much for Him to do. Surely we will love and trust Him more and more entirely every day, every hour. He well deserves it all.

Faith calls for the extremest simplicity; the utmost possible naturalness of speech and intercourse. Thus though it is good to have set times and regular seasons for prayer and for listening to God, it is by no means enough that we have such seasons. Human intercourse is rendered delightful by its spontaneity; by the welling up of warm affections whenever the crust of our ordinary life is penetrated by a friendly word, a kindly tone, or look, or by any other revelation of regard. Our beloved Lord is the nearest, dearest, tenderest friend we have; persistent, ceaseless, wonderfully considerate, and forever anticipating our possible desires. How natural then, how eminently suitable, that we should be breaking out at every turn in the road, with the sweet Psalmist of old: "I will praise Thee, O Lord, with my whole heart; I will shew forth all Thy marvelous works." Speak of the goodness of the Lord. Let others have the benefit of your experience. I am especially glad that you are meeting with so many mercies, and " seeing the hand of God so clearly in many of the minor details." Your faith will be confirmed, your love to Him increased. I do not at all believe that "in removing from E. to M. you have wandered away from Jesus." Man is as his real desire is; and I am sure that your real desire, like that of St. Paul, is to be "filled with the knowledge of His will, in all wisdom and spiritual understanding; to walk worthy of the Lord unto all pleasing; to be fruitful in every good work, and to increase in the knowledge of God." God's goodness to you, and your recognition of it, is as much a boon to me as to you. Are we not "joint-heirs with Christ?" Just so has He dealt with me, sending blessing upon blessing.

> "O Christ! He is the fountain,
> The deep sweet well of love."

So then tell your experience of this love. You surely wish to strengthen the faith of all His saints, as well as to convert sinners, therefore speak of what He has done and is doing for you. We do not want the experience of perfect people. It is the knowledge of what God has done for imperfect people, like ourselves, that touches us most nearly, that instructs us most effectively. But the utterance to others must be preceded by speaking to the Lord. Tell Him everything. Say to Him, Dear Lord, I delight in being in Thy hands. I have undoubting confidence in Thy management. Not for worlds would I take my matters into my own hands. Behold Thy servant; be it unto me even as Thou wilt. I see multitudes around me to whom Thou art giving a measure of success to which I do not even aspire. Be it so, dear Lord; I am content. Give what Thou wilt to whom Thou wilt, but give me Thy love. I dearly love Thee. I hunger, I thirst, I long, I pine for Thee, and for Thy likeness. Make haste to sanctify me. I do not see Thee, I cannot hear the sound of Thy footsteps; I cannot lay my hand on Thee: no matter, I know Thee. Thou art here, Thou art mine, and I am Thine. Blessed Comforter, I know Thee too. Thou dwellest with me, and in me; here in this heart. I have long ago thrown its door wide open to Thee. Ten thousand times I have offered Thee full and exclusive possession of its every hall, and nook, and corner. If there are any occupants here Thou dost not like, they are not here with my consent. I hate Thine enemies and mine with a perfect hatred. I pray Thee, turn them out. Of myself I am not strong enough to turn them out, nor wise, nor vigilant enough to keep them out. But if Thou wilt only give me clean riddance of them, I will bless Thee with my whole soul. Thou knowest, sweet Lord, that I long with insatiable longing to have every thought brought into perfect and ever enduring captivity to Thyself; whom not having seen I love; in whom, though now I see Thee not, yet believing, I rejoice with joy unspeakable, and full of glory. President Edwards says his custom was to talk with Jesus, to sing to Him, in a low tone, by himself. It is a blessed way to do. The best Christians I have ever known have been given to it. This is treating Him as real, and He gives in return real and most substantial tokens of His appreciation of such friendship.

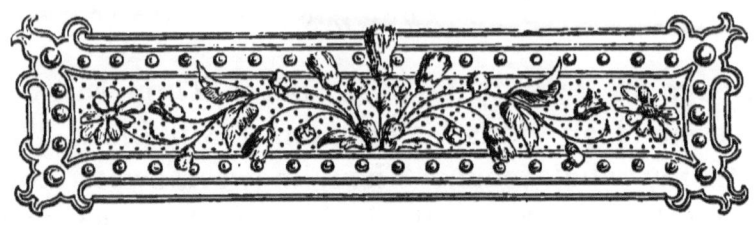

XXVIII.

ASPIRATION.

"Jesus saith unto him, Blessed are they that have not seen, and yet have believed."—JOHN xx. 29.

"Jesus, thou Joy of loving hearts!
Thou Fount of Life! Thou Light of men!
From the best bliss that earth imparts,
We turn unfilled to Thee again."

YOU are to believe that Jesus is ever with you because you have His word for it; only that, and nothing more. You have most unquestionably heard His voice, and opened the door of your heart to Him, and He has come in to you and dwells with you. And you have no right to invalidate His word, however much you may feel that you ought to confess your unworthiness. I often think that we can improve upon Peter's hasty, "Depart from me, for I am a sinful man, O Lord." I am a sinful man, therefore do not forsake me, Lord, for what can I do without Thee? It is the method of His loving-kindness to permit your moods, your ebb and flow of feeling in order to draw you more close to Himself. Consider what a boon He has bestowed on you in making you unable to live out of the sunlight of His love! How sad would be your condition, if you could be, as thousands are, easy and indifferent about it. Pant after Him if you will, and as much as you can; but also rest in Him; remembering His assurance, "Peace I leave with you; my peace I give unto you." We are ever apt to think that some one phase of spiritual life is the phase acceptable to our Lord. Whereas He has provided, and is ever so providing, as to secure the development of a many-sided love. To read Paul's outburst in Romans viii.: "Who shall separate us from the love of Christ?" or King David's, in Psalm cxlv.: "I will extol thee, my God, O King!" is indeed exhilarating; but not less profitable is it to turn to Psalm cxxxi., and in those precious words to breathe into His listening ear, "My soul is even as a weaned child." When we consider how great is the work of sanctification, which our Lord is carrying on, is it strange that we cannot measure the means which He is employing? Shall the thing formed and being formed, say to Him that formed it, Why hast Thou made me thus?

When "it is sometimes hard work to speak to Him," is it not that your desire is to speak in a way not compatible with your then present condition? Suppose you cannot employ the language of exultation, can you not use that of tender appeal? "Lord save, or I perish." "Dear Lord, I am a worm and no man." "Lord, I am Thine; poor, weak, feeble, sinful as I am, I am Thine, and only Thine. To whom else can I go?" And when you cannot talk at all, call to mind the beautiful illustration of the child too ill to speak, but who can and does now and then open his eyes to assure himself that the inclosing arms are his mother's; then shuts his eyes and rests content.

What you call your indolence and listlessness, is without doubt sheer physical exhaustion. There is as much piety and love in acquiescing in that, as in "subduing kingdoms." I do not believe Mary of Bethany was one of the great workers. The record says, "She sat at Jesus' feet and heard His word." That would harmonize with your capabilities; and I am sure He welcomes you there, especially on those days when "you find it almost impossible to speak to God or man." And, feeling confident that I know His mind in this, I will venture to assure you, that you cannot please Him better than in laying your weary head upon His shoulder.

You remember what my dear James said, of how "Locke on the Understanding" brought him the help he needed, when he could not make Dr. K. understand his perplexity. He needed to know the bounds of human thought. "I seemed to be in search of first principles; something to base my reflections upon. Locke supplies that want; shows me what is self-evident; what is capable of demonstration; and what must be settled by a balance of probabilities."

This morning M. gave utterance to a thought, very common, I fear, but which has not a shadow of foundation, strangely and most unhappily dropped into her mind by the unthinking, or not well-considered expression, of one whose earnest desire was to comfort her. The statement was, that "in heaven all the inhabitants were brothers and sisters." And the impression was, that there all family ties were obliterated. I can hardly conceive of a misconception — for such it assuredly is — more completely contrary to the teachings of our Lord; contrary to the blessed family relation which He created and gave to man as a most precious type of the heavenly life, and a constant incentive to press toward it. I had planned a much more earthly occupation for this hour, but this seems such a hurtful misrepresentation, I am unwilling to delay to record my protest against it, as a memorandum for another chapter which I trust our Lord may some day give me leave to write for the consolation of His troubled saints. I would begin with John xiii. 1, and show that Jesus' loving consideration for the necessities with which He endowed His creatures, is not to be so abridged: "Having loved His own which were in the world, He loved them to the end." Mindful of the loving hearts just about to be bereaved of their dearest Friend, He set Himself to provide for them the varied consolation which they would so much need. He gave them a love-feast without a precedent and without a parallel; not alone for those first disciples, but for every disciple, a memorial feast, to be frequently renewed, at which He would always sit with them. Let not your hearts be troubled, hitherto I have been visibly present with you, and your grief that I am to be so no longer, is natural. But I shall be none the less truly with you. You believe in God the Father, though He is not visible to the eye. As you believe in Him, so believe in me. Believe without a doubt. I am going to my Father. In His house are many mansions, various and peculiar, as are you, my beloved disciples, and suitable withal to the characteristics of their several tenants. If it had been otherwise I would have told you. As it is, I am going before you to prepare for each of you his appropriate dwelling. Understand me: I have been training you for your respective homes; and trust me, I will take care to fit those homes to the characteristics, and the tastes which I have been forming in you. Remember the words I have spoken to you, and be sure that in keeping these words you are making daily preparation for a blessed and glorious reunion. In your hearts I have implanted conjugal, parental, filial, and fraternal affection; each in its way an earnest of the love of heaven. And as you now comprehend these forms of love, I appeal to each of them, in sure token that your fidelity to me in them shall be rewarded to the full. To each of you I say with emphasis, "I thy Maker am thy husband." "I am thy Father." "A brother born for adversity." Children, I command to "obey and honor their parents;" "husbands to love their wives; and wives to love and honor their husbands." I remind you of the tenderness of a mother's love. And I have both commended to you, and illustrated for you, the sweets of friendship: "Now Jesus loved Mary and Martha and their brother Lazarus." "God is love." And nothing is so formative as love, nothing educates like love, "Love is the fulfilling of the law." What you will be when you enter heaven, will be in great part, what you have been made by love. How egregious, then, the error of those who infer from Matt. xxii. 30, that to "be as the angels of God," is to be stripped of all that individualizes the man, the woman, and the child; is to arrest the heart-currents of a lifetime.

14

XXIX.

WALKING WITH GOD.

> "Thy presence has a wondrous power!
> The sharpest thorn becomes a flower,
> And breathes a sweet perfume;
> Whate'er looked dark and sad before,
> With happy light shines silvered o'er
> There's no such thing as gloom."

YOU say that "in attempting to pray, you have never once had any conscious impression of the presence of the Divine Being."

So far as I have had the means of knowing, the number of those who uniformly have any conscious impression of the presence of the Lord, is small. One intelligent friend, of whom I made inquiry, said he viewed this consciousness as the fruit of a sensibility which is a gift, just as any of the talents we possess are the gift of God. This view seems to me to find a measure of confirmation in the aptitude we discover in ourselves to come to know some persons. It is in marked contrast with our backwardness, not to say impossibility, of knowing certain other persons. I suppose you feel this. And the quicker and finer the sensibility possessed, the more we should expect that attraction or repulsion to be strong. When we feel strongly attracted to any one we are quick to see and feel the qualities which represent to us the personality we admire and love. Not unfrequently we adopt those whom we have never seen on the testimony of mutual friends. We believe their testimony, and believing, embrace a personality which cannot be separated from the characteristics affirmed of them. If we can thus believe in our fellow-man, it does not appear that we may not in like manner, and with equal distinctness, believe what is affirmed of God, the witnesses being equally credible. If we have received in any considerable degree the characteristics commended by our Lord in His Sermon on the Mount, poverty of spirit, sympathy, compassion, meekness, purity, etc., we shall be quick to discern and to admire these in Him, and so the more we study the Scriptures which contain His illustrations of these graces, the more probable it would seem that our love through these would make Him near and real to us. I have been thinking how daily life must differ to the apprehension of persons unequally and differently endowed. Thus, for example, a dozen persons might travel on a summer's day from M. to New Haven. One might traverse the road with a drove of cattle before him, with no higher thought than of pasturage, and of the price to be gotten for his cattle. Another might pass over the same road thinking only of some case in law, or of some problem in metaphysics. Another with some humane purpose of obtaining a reasonable suffrage for freedmen. Still another with sweet meditations of Him who planted your happy people upon that pleasant Sound, and the great and wide sea beyond, the murmur of whose waves were sounding in his ear a glorious psalm, his eyes and his heart turning continually to the manifold works of God, and the loving-kindness that pervades them all. To one filled with such sensibility as God sometimes bestows, every foot of this road might contain an inspiration to extol the great Creator for facts and truths entirely unperceived by the men before and behind him. So it is in all the pilgrimage from the city of Destruction to Mount Zion. Men are variously affected by all the incidents of the way, "according to that a man hath, and not according to that he hath not."

It seems to me that much concern about how you ought to feel, when attempting to speak to your Lord, must distract your mind and hinder access to Him. Accept very simply and with thankfulness His grace to your young converts. Cut out work for them. Show them the relation between working for Him and growth in grace. And for further lessons, what can be sweeter or more hopeful than the utterance of the beloved John: "That which we have seen and heard, declare we unto you. And these things we write unto you that your joy may be full." And John the Baptist says: "Behold the Lamb of God. He is the true light which lighteth every man. As many as receive Him, to them He gives power to become the sons of God." The ability to receive the revelation of Himself is, you see, the gift of God. Now if He sees fit to withhold for a time the happy realization you desire, may it not be, must it not be, that there is in this withholding some gracious design? One thing much to be desired is this: that we should learn to follow Christ for what He is in Himself, rather than for what He may bestow on us. In studying the Bible for this purpose, we discover what Christ is in His dealings with others. In so studying we pursue our inquiry without bias from self-interest. We learn to trust Jesus Himself. Our minds are turned away from peculiarities of personal experience, our own or others'. We are encouraged to take each word and act appropriate to our needs and uses as actually spoken by our Lord to us personally. In proportion as we dismiss all worldly wisdom, and are content with being but babes, does it become practicable to sit at Jesus' feet and learn of Him.

You seem to decline to take the full benefit of the faith you have, because what Jesus has given you is so simple, so intelligible, and has come to you with so little that is startling. You did not think the kingdom of God would come in that way. You are not the first by many thousands, that has had this thought. Simple belief in Jesus, taking Him at His word, rings no bells, fires no cannon, makes no noise of any kind, but just believes, and goes on. Depend upon it, you need nothing but simply to believe that our Lord has called you, does call you, and is calling you, every moment; and that you have heard, have followed, and do now follow Him, from day to day, from hour to hour. Would you like an angel to speak from heaven, and say to you: "E. you are a believer, accepted and beloved of Jesus?" It would not help you a particle. It would be a hindrance. Because, what He requires, and what you need, is faith in Him; not faith in an angel. Unconsciously you are asking for some substitute for faith in your Lord. Do you not see that in His word Jesus comes straight to you, and says to you, "My dear child, give me your confidence, your love, your heart. Do I not deserve it? Have I not revealed myself to thee as no one else has ever done? Have I not given you a pen picture; a portrait of myself portrayed in God's own pure light? Have I not held it up to your view from your infancy. Is any part of it faint, dim, or in any way obscure? Was ever meekness and gentleness like mine? Was ever pity and compassion? Was ever purity and peace-making? Was ever heavenly aspiration like mine? You admire heroism; was I not persecuted even unto death? You admire patient endurance; when I was reviled, did I ever revile again? When the grossest insults and obloquy were heaped upon me, was ever a word, or act, or look of retaliation heard, or seen? Were not my last words, Father, forgive them, for they know not what they do? For what further evidence do you wait? You have not only Moses and the Prophets; you have the Psalmists, the Evangelists, and the Apostles. Above all, you have the Holy Ghost, the Comforter. He dwells with you and in you. Every day of your life He takes the things of God and of Christ and shows them to you. He is my representative; He is with you on purpose to redeem my assurance that you should be a gainer by my returning to the Father." Do you not think, that if you believed all this, it would make you happy? Then believe it; simply believe it, for it is entirely true. Do not fly off to any considerations of feeling. Irrespective of all such considerations, it is simply true; and you ought to believe it, and take the good of it. I say ought, yes indeed you ought; you owe it to yourself; you owe it to your husband; you owe it to your parishioners; you owe it to your fellow-creatures everywhere; above all, you owe it to our dear Lord Jesus Christ, who loved you, gave Himself for you, and ever liveth to make intercession for you. Take Jesus' words, John xiv. 13, 14, and xv. 7, and hear His own voice speaking to you. Believe and trust Him entirely, lovingly, thankfully. This is heart-sight of Jesus. The oftener you do this, the clearer and sweeter will be your vision of Him.

XXX.

PROVING ALL THINGS.

"We daily walk the crowded street,
  Nor heed the sky above us;
We seldom say to those we meet
  That there is One who loves us.
O weak in trust, and dim in sight!
  When will ye heed the teaching,
That Heaven is never out of sight,
  Nor God beyond our reaching?"

THE persons whose experiences make you reject or disparage your own, are made and fitted for another sphere, and not for yours. Never mind them, but turn to Jesus, and submit your thoughts and solicitudes to Him; not doubtfully, as if allowing the question, How can He possibly be concerned in matters so small as mine? Your affairs are such as He has been pleased to provide for you; and being yours they are of prime importance to you. You have His own permission and command, "Call upon me in the day of trouble, and I will deliver thee; and thou shalt glorify me. I will guide thee with mine eye." It seems to me as if He had said: I know your modesty, you need not cry very loud, I am not far away, I shall hear your every whisper. I will hasten to your relief.

You are distressed because "you have not an all-pervading sense of sin." You have heard, as I have often heard, the characteristic and oft repeated utterances of certain well meaning men, who do not consider that some things appropriate enough to themselves, growing out of their own peculiarities, may not befit the conditions and needs of others. I have known men truly and very earnest to be useful, steeped to the lips in self-complacency; quite conscious too of their sinfulness in this, filled with "an all-pervading sense of sin," — and why should they not be? But are we thence to assume that their neighbors, who have no such temptation, ought to employ the same language? Your easily besetting sin is not self-complacency; but rather, through excessive contemplation of your well known shortcomings, despondency. Fixing your attention upon your own failures, you unconsciously under-estimate the atonement which Christ your Lord has made. I think I might properly say, you have a too "pervading sense of sin;" since it invades and more or less obscures the movements of the Holy Spirit upon your mind and heart. Do not forget what St. Paul says of the effect of being in Christ. "There is therefore now no condemnation to them which are in Christ Jesus, who walk not after the flesh but after the Spirit. For the law of the spirit of life in Christ Jesus, hath made me free from the law of sin and death." To clutch, then, at "an all-pervading sense of sin," may be a strange perversion and rejection of your privilege; which is to grasp with unyielding tenacity the covenant of grace, and the remission of sins which the blood of Christ has secured to you. I have often heard obligation to agony in prayer urged upon believing, trusting Christians, in a fashion strangely inconsistent with our Lord's own teaching. He says: "Ask and ye shall receive." "Whatsoever ye shall ask in my name, that will I do. If ye shall ask anything in my name, I will do it." "When ye pray believe that ye receive, and ye shall have." "If ye then, being evil, know how to give good gifts to your children, how much more shall your Heavenly Father give the Holy Spirit to them that ask Him." Assuredly it may be well, and most proper, to say to those who are slumbering over their highest obligations: Awake and call upon your God; agonize to attain deliverance from your most criminal insensibility to the claims of your God. But to lash to a frenzy of further supplication, those whose special sin is that they do not accept the peaceful trust and joy in the Lord which Jesus proffers, is an almost unpardonable perversion and abuse of the commission our Lord gives to those whom He has sent, saying, "Comfort ye my people, saith your God. Speak ye comfortably to Jerusalem, and cry unto her that her warfare is accomplished, that her iniquity is pardoned." Alas! how true it is,

"We seldom say to those we meet,
That there is One who loves us."

And the reason for this omission, we may well believe is our own sinful insensibility to His love. We should agonize to surmount and forever put away this insensibility of unbelief, this obstinacy of disregard to His assurance, "I have loved thee with an everlasting love." Has the sum of His love ever yet been told?

I have sometimes been informed that I failed to make proper recognition of "the terrors of the Lord." I could only say in reply, that I wait constantly and only upon God according to Psalm lxii., and take thankfully what the Lord sends. I acknowledged that I might be unconsciously backward in many ways, but I could not recognize "the terrors" till He showed them to me. I could give to others only what I had received. I had received a very sweet and controlling sense of the love of God. I perceived that people generally did not care as much for that as for terrors; I was very sorry for it, but I could not quite feel to blame that He had given me a happier experience, even if it was less influential. I have found reason to question if the superior power of terrors be not more apparent than real; and it has occurred to me, that with my limited strength, a dispensation of love was more congruous with my commission, and compatible with my capabilities for usefulness, than the thunders of Sinai. Under the precious impulses of the former I could go steadily on for an indefinite period, and try to make up by continuous and even working for lack of the power which I could admire in others, but could find no way to acquire. I used to feel troubled about it, before I saw all this. I am troubled no longer. It seems probable to me, that with your delicate frame, you will have to content yourself with a like resignation. Fortunately we are to give account to God for what we have, and not for what we have not received. My own experience persuades me that a love of Jesus which is controlling, is a surer and more efficient power than fear; and we know that "perfect love casteth out fear." A thread is better than a cable, if it draws that which is to be drawn, because a child may use it. "The beauty and attractiveness of Jesus," kept in sight, is more prevailing than gravitation. The doubts of those who doubt this, recommend them to our pity and our prayers: as arguments, or as grounds for judicial decisions, they are valueless. Let us take pains to show young converts that sin consists in insensibility to "the meekness and gentleness of Christ;" in carelessness about His work, in indifference to the salvation of others; in self-sparing, and selfishness in any form. If "most of your Christian friends have attained something which you do not possess," it is no less true that God has freely bestowed on you something which multitudes of professing Christians lack, namely, that hunger and thirst which is the sure earnest of being filled. "Wait, I say, on the Lord." Your capacity to receive is being daily and hourly enlarged. "Fear not, little one, it is your Father's good pleasure to give you the kingdom," after you have suffered a while.

XXXI.

HOPE DEFERRED.

> "Why should I murmur? For the sorrow
>   Thus only longer-lived would be;
> Its end may come, and will, to-morrow,
>   When God has done His work in me;
> So I say, trusting, 'As God will!'
> And trusting to the end, hold still."

LET me share a pleasant thought with you. I was first thinking, another day's work lies before me; hard work, not naturally agreeable to me; work consuming time and strength; and so absorbing as to leave no time, or strength, or mental force for what seems best worth the while, for an immortal. And then, in an instant, I thought and said, It is all right, Lord, I see it all. This is Thy way of answering my most earnest prayer for holiness in order to usefulness. I perfectly understand, that in crossing all my natural preferences, Thou art giving me my heart's desire and prayer. How many years I have been praying this prayer! And never for a moment hast Thou lost sight of it, or failed to fashion the desired results. For twenty, thirty, forty years, has the prayer gone up, and I have watched and listened, and seen no sight, heard no sound, met with no startling intervention. But, in the depths of my heart, and through all my soul, I have the serene and full conviction, that the unseen, unheard answer, has been coming every day, every hour, every moment. "What a Friend we have above!" Now I like to tell you this, because, as He has been dealing with me, so He has been and is dealing with thee. How plainly it marks the sphere and work of faith: "Whom having not seen we love; in whom, though now we see Him not, yet believing, we rejoice with joy unspeakable and full of glory." You have been distressing yourself under a misapprehension into which we all fall, that were we praying most to the purpose we should be conscious of it; and also assured of immediate progress. No! it is in the absence of such evidence we are driven to Christ, and to His Word, asking ever with tender and tremulous solicitude, Lord, am I right? "Will the Lord cast off forever? Will He be favorable no more? Is His mercy clean gone forever? Doth His promise fail for evermore?" No! God hath not forgotten to be gracious. His grace has pervaded all His silence; and in due time, in the best time, in the fullness of time, this blessed truth will fill the soul with its radiance as when the sun shineth in his strength. I see and feel it constantly, and it makes my peace like a river, and like the fullness of the sea; and never is it more full and serene than when "He weakens my strength in the way;" so you will find it. When there is no sun or stars in the spiritual firmament, there is nothing for us but to turn to His chart, which is His word, and take His way-mark promises as our safe and certain guide.

You do well to be very solicitous to please Jesus; which, by the way, proves that you realize Him, your oft renewed protest to the contrary notwithstanding. What an ingenious soul you are in making out a case against yourself! You are perplexed because the multiplied labors, thrown upon you by the revival, leave you no undistracted time for prolonged reading and praying. But our Lord calls upon you to do only what you are capable of doing; and He calls you to use the best judgment you have about that. This much is plain: the work before you is God's work; He brought it to you. He has made its importance so palpable that you cannot put it from you; you feel that it must be done. Now, how would you act towards your mother under like circumstances? "Mother, I delight in doing anything for you, and whatever you bring me, I shall do, to the best of my ability; and I know that when in filling my hands with work for you, you leave me less time to talk with you, and to listen to you, you will not suspect me of any indifference, or voluntary absence from your chamber." So much confidence have you in your mother. Can you not trust Jesus as far? Besides, each word you speak for Jesus, to one of your inquirers, is an act of coöperation with Him which you cannot separate from prayer, without some strange perversity of unbelief. Hold yourself to the recognition of the fact, that He is in very deed with you and in you, in it all. Certainly you were never in the secrecy of your chamber nearer to Jesus than you are when so employed. Will He blame you, think you, when He so multiplies your labors that you can find time and strength only for ejaculatory prayers? You say, "I know I could rise earlier in the morning." I take the liberty to question that. I do not think you could. I am quite sure you ought not. It is true our Lord does place us sometimes in circumstances, in which, for a time, usually a very brief time, we are compelled to do more than we are well able to do. But generally, I suspect, a few days' work, followed up, is more acceptable to Him than overworking; and evidently it is the best economy for man and beast. No friend can adjust the balance for you; your scales are too fine for that. The Master has given you your judgment, and expects you to use it. Certainly He has given you an unmistakable intimation that you please Him; and I think you should accept it with all thankfulness. Were you indifferent to prayer, and to communion with Jesus in His Word, you might have reason for solicitude. But such is not the case. You are so far from being indifferent, that you are making yourself altogether too anxious. Another thought: Not a few Christians make a superstition of regular and set readings of the Bible and prayers; and especially of reading a full chapter or more. I have heard Sunday-school teachers proclaim to their scholars that by reading two or three chapters each week-day, and five on Sunday, they could accomplish the praiseworthy task of getting through the Bible in a year. Now I find that I never read the Bible so profitably as when some single verse, or two verses, get such hold of me that for days, weeks, and sometimes months, I cannot consent to give them up, or to read any other verses. Really earnest, growing Christians will neither, on the one hand, catch at slight excuses for omitting or shortening regular daily devotions; nor, on the other hand, make a rule so inflexible as to substitute daily reading and prayer for growing love and obedience to Christ. One thing more and more impresses me, the need of all this discipline of perplexity, because the transforming of such creatures as we are into the image of Jesus is such an immense matter. Take that view of it, and account every new perplexity new evidence that our beloved Lord is using the attrition of trial to make you more like Himself. I am sure that this is the true interpretation of it. I have realized it to be so during the two months past beyond what I have ever done before. And the sweet peace this realization gives, is greater than I can tell you. Evidently our Lord is answering your prayers abundantly. Do not trouble or perplex yourself because your young converts are traveling a shorter road than yourself. That was just what I found in dear "Orient's" case. She learned in two years what cost me twenty. Why should He not so prepare one who was so soon to be caught up to be with the Lord. Besides, "we are made a spectacle to angels;" and they are instructed in the grace of God, when they find us blessing God that our pupils are doing better than we have done.

Beyond a doubt your sometime-worry arises in no small part from your not realizing how perfectly safe it is for you just to assume the unwavering love Jesus bears you, and so to give up all care of yourself to Him. He will take care of you; full care. He knows you by name. It is not so much "a deeper consecration you need," as a simple belief in the consecration you have already made; that Jesus accepts both it and you. You are not to worry yourself about an ideal consecration, which you conceive of, as a possibility, but which you can in no way lay hold of, as a reality. That consecration may possibly be somebody's duty, but it is not yours. I do not think "Jesus would be more real to you if you sought Him oftener in the closet;" your trouble does not, I think, lie there. But you need while about the common occupations of life often to remind yourself, "Jesus is real, is mine, and I am His; He has taken me just as I am, and He is making me just what He wishes me to be. Every day He is setting this work forward. He says it." John xiii. 1; xvii. 19.

Thanks to Brother G. for his assurance that he can make use of me in M., and I echo your desire that I may come to you in the fullness of the blessing of the Gospel of Christ. I mean to ask the members of my three Bible-classes to make intercession to that end. Upborne by such a cloud of prayer, I shall confidently expect the Divine approval and blessing on the endeavor.

You ask what I think of our friends knowing in Heaven of our on-goings here. I have the strongest persuasion that they do know, for Jesus knows; and they having awaked in His likeness, are in perfect and intimate sympathy with Him; His cares are their cares, and their cares His cares. It must therefore be His pleasure to tell them much that they must wish to know. You remember Bishop Butler holds that an order of things existing, is to be presumed to continue, unless there is probable cause for its discontinuance; unless it can be shown that there is in the change that which forbids the expectation of its continuance. Now there is in the change, which we call death, nothing to forbid the expectation of the continuance of those powers and interests upon which death has no power. Our affections obviously must survive, because there is nothing in death adapted to arrest the affections themselves, though it has power to arrest that manifestation of them which is seen in the working of the physical powers.

XXXII.

JESUS ONLY.

"Ho! thou traveler on life's highway,
　Moving carelessly along,
Pausing not to watch the shadows
　Lowering o'er the mighty throng!
Stand aside and mark how feebly
　Some are struggling in the fight,
Turning on thee wistful glances,
　Begging thee to hold the light."

AT Guilford a bright, sunny-faced young girl got into the car and took her seat with another less sunny, about the same age, in the seat next mine. The first looked so like some of your bright young Christians, I presently turned to her and asked, " Do you love Jesus ? "

"Yes, sir ;" was the quick, bright answer ; and her eyes sparkled with the heart in them.

" How long have you loved Him ? "

" Two years, sir."

" And you have n't lost the sound of His voice ? "

" No, sir."

" And you do not intend to lose it ? "

" No, sir."

" And you never need, my dear child, if you will only keep near Him."

I then turned to the other: "And do you love Jesus, too?"

"I don't profess to."

"Ah, that's sad." I said; "and you want to be happy too; but you can't be truly till you love Him." I found they were both going to West M.; the first to teach school; and I engaged her to look after the other. She said she would.

My heart is so full this morning that I must let out some of it. I woke at half-past five, full of love, and praise, and prayer. The sense of our dear Lord's goodness and love was overpowering. I thought of how much He had been giving me in M. and since. I prayed for you all; and then for the dear class I am to meet this afternoon. Then I wrote to dear Dr. C., telling him how I rejoiced in his sermon on Sunday morning; especially in what he said of simple faith in God; of reliance on His Word; and of no need to see signs and wonders. I was peculiarly impressed because of an incident which occurred on Saturday evening at my dear friend D.'s. His brother, a convert of a few weeks only, drew me towards him, saying, "Now tell me all about your work at M."

"Well," I said, "I had a blessed visit; I enjoyed every moment. Brother G. took me to a half a dozen or more districts of his wide town. My heart was full and running over. Such a sea of up-turned young and older faces! and such attention! a soul in every face!"

"But did you lead any one to Christ?" I was dumb. The question took me at unawares. Had I been in Dr. C.'s vein I should have shouted in reply, "When God leads up the sun, is there any light?" Lead any one to Christ? Aye, I led them all to Christ! Nay, better than that, I brought Christ to them; and offered Him to every soul, on His own commission; free as air, and full of grace and truth and love.

Recognizing the fact, that there are some who dishonor the Master through the absence of all expectation that He will redeem His pledge: "My Word shall not return unto me void, but it shall accomplish that which I please, and it shall prosper in the thing whereto I sent it," I must think that others offend, not less, in ignoring His declaration: "By grace ye are saved, through faith; and that not of yourselves; it is the gift of God." I could sympathize with the King of Israel, and demand, Am I God, to kill and to make alive, that this man expects me to recover men from the leprosy of sin? My commission is to preach the gospel to every creature. Towards this I did my best endeavor.

The sense of Christ's presence, and of His love, was so near and so sweet I could not help repeating to myself in the cars, Sweet Jesus! oh, how good Thou art! How shall I ever thank Thee as I ought and would?

> "The love of Jesus, what it is,
> None but His loved ones know."

Coming from the cars, homeward, I met my friend C. who exacted a promise that I would preach in L. Street Chapel on Sunday. My text was that precious one, "Behold I stand at the door and knock." At the close of the service Mr. and Mrs. C. rushed up, eager to know, "Had I been reading Jean Ingelow's "Brothers and a Sermon?" The sermon is on this same text. I had not then read it. I have since. Her sermon is a gem; I have rarely, if ever, met with any so beautiful; and so forceful and persuasive too. Who and what can she be? Could any but an earnest Christian worker, and a rare poet, write that sermon? I know not. Alas! for the possibilities. I recall with sorrow the o'er-true declaration of another accomplished authoress: "It is one thing to depict a useful life, and quite another to live it." One of my early morning impressions, before I had risen from my pillow, was, Jesus means to convert W. Remember His covenant with you for your children. And then I fell to praying with a vehemence I could never attain to before, that He would make a work so deep, so thorough, as to be a wonder among wonderful conversions. And I think He will.

I do not remember if I told you that when R. L. passed us on Friday evening, she whispered in my ear, "I see a ray of light." It made me anticipate the result you report. Set her and all the rest of your young converts to work for Jesus. We must have a new kind of Christians for these wonderful times, working Christians.

The impression of the young lady you quote, that "this is her last call," has had many precedents. I should feel as you do, deeply solicitous for her, but in no haste to conclude that this is not the pitying Saviour's way of touching her too deeply to permit her to evade the call. No doubt "Satan does suggest all manner of discouragements;" but in suggesting such an one as this, even with the imputation of hardness and injustice to God, he would most likely overshoot his mark.

It is very pleasant to learn what you say of the captain. God's word is sure, as to His promises; sure too as to the effect of His word.

If I never hear of a case of conversion from the use of my little books from now to the end of my life, I shall expect, without a doubt, to find many when we get home. Only believe, dear sister, and you shall know that your labor is not, and never shall be, in vain in the Lord. You will have a host of sheaves. Tell Jesus everything. Nothing is little in His sight that contributes to the peace and well-being of His saints. Your smallest solicitudes He gave you, that you might bring them to Him. That is His way of keeping you an intimate and tenderly loving friend. "Oh how great is Thy goodness, which Thou hast laid up for them that fear Thee; which Thou hast wrought for them that trust in Thee before the sons of men." Say to Jesus, "Set me as a seal upon Thine heart; as a seal upon Thine arm; for love is strong as death." "I sleep but my heart waketh."

XXXIII.

FEED MY LAMBS.

"*Lovest* thou me? Feed my lambs."—JOHN xxi. 16.

"My sole possession is Thy love;
In earth beneath, or heaven above,
I have no other store;
And though with fervent suit I pray,
And importune Thee night and day,
I ask Thee nothing more."

THANKS for your kind note. I am indeed rejoiced to have been of any use to Mrs. M., and sorry not to have become acquainted with your little K. Nothing could mar such a visit. The throat difficulty was the most serious obstacle. But when God is about to confer some uncommon blessing He usually begins by reminding me that I have nothing, and am nothing. He has taken away my pen; that is, disabled the brain that used to employ it; and now, when I had just begun to think that a wide door was opening to me in lay-preaching, He has laid His hand upon my throat too. The inference all past experience warrants me in drawing is, that He means to purify me, and in so doing greatly to enlarge my usefulness. So have I ever found it, and so will you. I have promised a friend to go on Thursday, the State Fast, to Tewkesbury, and preach in the morning, and address the young people in the afternoon. He almost compelled me, in spite of my suspicion that I have not yet got back voice enough. But I have fallen in love with the work, and do not like to lose it, if I may be permitted to keep it. I am full of Father G.'s mind, that our Lord has given you a very great blessing, in giving you the care of those young people, and in giving you their love. Certainly He could give you no more sure token of His love than this. I have just had a call from a dear lamb whom the Good Shepherd intrusted to me in our country sojourn last summer. "Oh, how good He is!"

I finished Romans with my Tuesday class yesterday afternoon. That class has been larger of late; from twenty to twenty-five. In the evening I took my friend D.'s class at his house, he being engaged to preach at Salem church. How good it is to have so many blessed opportunities! My heart is made very glad by them.

I am afraid you are over-working yourself, beyond all reason, beyond all right. Faith is the antidote to a fevered anxious hurry, even to do good. Our dear Lord is most mercifully considerate of these frames of ours. He knows that they are but dust; and I am perfectly sure that we honor Him by refusing to be driven beyond our strength.

I bless God that He enabled you to hear the tender whisper of our dear Lord Jesus at His table,

"This is my body broken for you." Your remark, "I don't know how to deal with happy Christians, so well as with troubled ones," greatly interests me. What a soul-satisfying comment this supplies; and interpretation too, to your experiences hitherto. The happy Christians can more easily do without you. Your prayer was just right; not a bit "too bold." I am sure the Good Shepherd prompted it, and that He will gloriously answer it. Do not fear to renew it, and press it as often as He suggests and inspires it, which will be as often as it comes to you. And the desolation with which you rose yesterday morning, probably, — I might say certainly, — was the harbinger of the gift desired. Follow your impulses to believe wholly. Do not distrust them. There is no danger that you will believe too much, or that you will expect too much. Take this thought for your comfort: Every hour you struggle on, "faint yet pursuing," hungering for Jesus, yet not rebelling or murmuring because He keeps you waiting; you give Him a treasure of loyal love far, far beyond the offerings of one who has no such aching insatiable void. "How precious are thy thoughts unto me, O God;" thoughts of Thine absolutely perfect knowledge; Psalm cxxxix. 1, that Thou knowest my very thought; ver. 2, thoughts of Thy nearness; ver. 3, and protection, descending to the smallest details; ver. 4, and steadying me with Thy hand; ver. 5, filling me with ineffable peace in the joyful assurance of Thy presence; ver. 6–12, thoughts of Thy foresight and painstaking; ver. 13–16, and Thy generous intentions in my behalf, namely, sure deliverance from the wicked, and the still more momentous deliverance from every thought and way not agreeable to Thy pure will.

XXXIV.

HOPE.

> " How few from their youthful day
> Look into what their life may be,
> Painting the visions of the way
> In colors soft, and bright, and free.
> How few who to such paths have brought
> The hopes and dreams of early thought!
> For God, through ways they have not known
> Will lead His own."

I HAVE written N. a letter which perhaps her patience will not hold out to read. It has turned out to be the germ of a little thing entitled "Difficulties of Converts."

I thought of you and prayed for you yesterday at the Lord's table. I have no doubt you had a profitable "Communion." I wish you could have been present on Friday evening in our chapel. Mr. D. was in the desk, and his text was, "The Master has come and calleth for thee." Quite a number stopped after the service for personal conversation.

Your letter is a precious letter. I cannot thank our dear Lord enough for it. But you are only in the beginning of the feast, "Thou shalt see greater things than these." His precious word will open to you more and more; and your love to Him will expand like a flower in the sun. I send you my string of "Difficulties." Possibly you may recognize some of them. While I was finishing it, it occurred to me that some of H.'s might have been added. But I was thankful that the thought did not come sooner, for I had grappled with as many as I had strength for. Yesterday noon I was at Mr. D.'s for a moment; and asked him if he knew "Brothers and a Sermon," by Jean Ingelow? He did not, but went to the book-case and got the volume. I told him to read it to his wife, and it would teach him new pathos in preaching. In the evening our seamstress went to the U. church to hear him. When she came home she told Mrs. K., she never heard a minister in all her life she liked so much; and his text was, "Behold I stand at the door and knock."

It was not to be supposed that the bitter enemy of God and man would see you slipping out of his cruel net, into the very peace of Jesus, and not make one more effort to entangle you. But comfort yourself with David's consolation, Psalm cxviii. 6, "The Lord is on my side; I will not fear. What can man [or Satan] do unto me?" You must needs have these ups and downs, until by patient waiting on the Lord you are established. And you know that "After you have suffered a while, He will establish, strengthen, settle you." These sufferings are hard to bear; but they are not therefore unprofitable. On the contrary they are yielding the peaceable fruits of righteousness; developing in you graces not to be acquired in any other way, bringing you ever into closer sympathy and oneness of experience with our beloved Lord; as in Hebrews v. 8, "Who learned obedience [in spirit; that is, docility,] by the things which He suffered." A word about the old trouble, of not being able to find, or realize your Saviour. To have a vivid and continuous sense of His presence is very, very sweet and desirable; but when we have not that, we still hold a power of immense worth; the power, namely, to insist with ourselves, thus: Jesus is, however I· may think or feel, or fail to feel. And He is all that I ever in my happiest moments believed Him to be. He is not changed a particle by my fluctuations. He is true, tender, and constant still. Still, "I am my Beloved's; and my Beloved is mine." "For whom have I in heaven but Thee? and there is none upon earth whom I desire beside Thee." What if I do walk in a thick fog? Thou, dear Jesus, art with me in the fog; nay, Thyself hast brought the fog about me, that I may walk in it, hand in hand with Thee. Lead me where Thou wilt. Led by Thee I cannot go amiss. It is heaven to be with Thee, be it in deepest, densest fog, or elsewhere. I do not say that such resolves will always and at once lift us above the fog and the sorrow. But I do say, that such is the tendency; and that they will surely contribute much towards it. Is it not obvious to you that such is the design of these trystings? Knowing the love of Jesus, can you doubt it? To me it is not "hard to believe that just that utter desolation may be God's way of teaching us lessons of humility, faith, and dependence." True while we are in that desolation it is hard to believe anything, except as we instantly throw all the force we can summon from will, and all we can get by asking, into a renewed act of giving ourselves to Jesus, and trusting in Him. Sometimes, as I go around the house, the last thing at night, to make all fast, in the multiplicity of my thoughts I do my office mechanically, and cannot answer the question, Did I turn that lock or not? Next time I give it a vigorous turn, and say to myself, "There, now I have locked that door, whether I can remember it or not." Can you take advantage of such an illustration, and give yourself to Jesus with such strength of decision, that you can add, There, now I have given myself all away to Him at any rate, let come what doubts may come. Have you never said to yourself in the midst of a hateful dream, in the slumbers of the night, "It is only a dream; I will not heed it." I lately saw an excellent suggestion; that "before going to sleep we firmly resolve, Now if I happen to have such a dream, I will remind myself that it is only a dream." I believe in such power of the will. You see the point; will you not act upon it the next time the occasion offers? Resolve never to give in to any temptation; never to doubt that whatever comes is simply your Heavenly Father's discipline, and is sure to "work out for you a far more exceeding and eternal weight of glory.".

Rest in the deep conviction, that the course of education chosen for us by the Holy Spirit, is not only safe, but infinitely more profitable than any course our self-sparing might incline us to; even if we had the wisdom with which to choose. And so we will pray for strength to endure; for " Behold we count them happy which endure."

XXXV.

COMING VICTORY.

> "I 've wrestled on toward heaven,
>   'Gainst storm and wind and tide;
> Now like a weary traveler
>   That leaneth on his guide,
> Amid the shades of evening,
>   While sinks life's lingering sand,
> I hail the glory dawning
>   From Immanuel's land."

ABOUT "regular employments for different hours;" your desire to make the most and the best of life, will prompt you to try many experiments. Many of them will not work; but the endeavor will do you good, provided you do not overtax your strength. In 1833 I mapped out the day in hours and half hours, and tried to assign its appropriate work to each section of the day and hour. No doubt the endeavor had its uses; but the thing could not be sustained for any length of time; not even then, when I had much more than now the control of time and opportunities. As for "ignorance," it is just the same with me, I presume each of us finds abundant reason to believe that no one else can be so ignorant. But trying, despite the acknowledged ignorance, to do what we can, is a blessed privilege, and a most valuable discipline. I do not think I should wish to have less consciousness of ignorance, whatever might be my actual acquisitions; it is so safe, and so true, the realization that "I'm a poor sinner and nothing at all." We will travel on hand in hand, conscious of innumerable short-comings "in minor matters," and in larger matters; so walking humbly with our Lord; but all the more sturdily clinging to His assurance that "if we confess our sins, He is faithful and just to forgive us our sins, and to cleanse us from all unrighteousness."

"What shall I say of a person who tried to pray in the morning, and was so impressed with the idea that she was mocking God, that she gave it up; and then tried again; and then again, four or five times?" I should say to her: Poor soul! see here a verification of Bunyan's fidelity to the facts of Christian experience! Satan trying to quench the heavenly fire; and behind the wall the Holy One pouring on oil. I would say, Beloved, have faith in the Holy One. They that are with thee are more than all they that are against thee. I have a message for thee from the Master: "Fear not little one; it is your Father's good pleasure to give you the kingdom. Satan hath desired to have thee, that he may sift thee as wheat; but I have prayed for thee, that thy faith fail not. Be not anxiously fearful; I have conquered Satan, I myself was tempted by him, therefore I permit thee to be thus tempted, in token of my special love. I permit you to drink of my cup, that your fellowship with me may be the more intimate. Tell me, my child, if you can, What could I do for you that I have not done, to assure you of my quenchless love? Be not faithless; but trust me despite all appearances. I am but testing thy faith, and illustrating the power of even such a little one as thou art, to overcome, through the grace of God which is in thee, to make all men see what is the fellowship of the mystery, — the mysterious and wonderful fellowship, — which from the beginning of the world hath been hid in God; to the intent that now unto the principalities and powers in heavenly places might be known by the Church, of which you are a part, the manifold wisdom of God; the love too; the inexhaustible riches of love, from which nothing can separate you."

XXXVI.

PEACE.

" For the mountains shall depart, and the hills be removed; but my kindness shall not depart from thee, neither shall the covenant of my peace be removed, saith the Lord that hath mercy on thee." — Is. liv. 10.

" How sweetly parts the Christian's sun,
Just like the summer monarch set,
'Midst cloudless skies his journey done,
To rise in brighter regions yet.
Oh where the Christian ends his days,
Lingers a lovely line of rays,
That speaks his calm departure blest,
And promises to those who gaze,
The same beatitude of rest."

IT may be that some one of our Lord's little ones having read this record of a hungry child, — so she often called herself, — will be wishing to ask me, Were your expectations realized? Did she ever attain the experience she thirsted for?

You shall hear. As I have already indicated, she was one of the Lord's good shepherds. Not long before she was called to her heavenly home she wrote the following letter to a timid believer, who had been long an invalid. Not having strength to write another, she desired a friend to make a copy of this and ask me to accept it as though written to me, that I might know her state.

"My dear Friend: For many weeks I have been waiting to feel strong enough to write you. I have thought a great deal of you, and very tenderly, and have been longing to be permitted to lead you into the quiet rest which the Lord has given to me.

"Now do not be surprised to hear me say this, and begin at once to say that I have received some new light, or come into some marvelous experience, and that I have left you far behind. Not a bit of it; but I think I do know more of what trusting in God means, than I used to know. When my kind doctor first told me that I had a fatal disease upon me, and that I must at once drop everything, and care first of all for my health, in that same hour I believe I did 'drop everything,' spiritual burdens as well as temporal. I had been tugging away at myself for months and years, trying to grow better; trying, I rather think, to make myself of some account in God's sight. I was always looking forward to the time when I should be more prayerful, more diligent, more consecrated, and then God would be pleased with me, and I would hope I was His child. There it was, you see, just nothing but self-righteousness after all. But my doctor's words made me feel that I carried about a volcano that might at any moment end my earthly existence. In one little hour I was brought face to face with the fact that my doing, of whatever sort, was nearly ended; and that I might have no more time in which to finish my work in this world, or to get ready for another.

"I was not alarmed or troubled, though greatly surprised. But my first thought was, 'Well I am in the Lord's hands, and I know it now.' And my next, the prayer, 'Lord take me; I give myself to Thee just as I am. I can do nothing more to make myself better; I can never be more fit to come to Thee than in this moment.'. And I think the Lord must have heard that prayer. No rustle of angelic wings stirred the air. No visible revelation appeared to me. No deep joy flowing into my soul, made me feel that my prayer was accepted, and that I was just taken up into the Good Shepherd's arms. But very quietly and calmly, without a wish to have anything different, I sat that long Sabbath afternoon, and talked with a dear friend of the message the Lord had sent me. How strange it all was; in the morning, not feeling strong, to be sure, but with no suspicion that anything ailed me beyond a temporary weakness; in the afternoon sitting already by the bank of the river that separates us from our heavenly home. Well, the quiet calmness that came to me in that hour, my Lord's own gift to me, has never left me. 'It is the Lord's doing, and it is marvelous in our eyes.' I have no fears for the future, so far as my sickness is concerned; nor any wish that I know of, as to the length of my stay here. This you know cannot be any human experience; for I have much to make life pleasant to me. Nor have I a longing desire to depart. All that I put into the Lord's hands once for all. And He has given me grace to leave it there. Jesus is not any more real to me than He was before. I don't feel that I love Him better, or am nearer to Him. I should be glad to do so; but I don't fight any longer because I cannot do this. I find I can trust if things are not as I think they ought to be; or as I wish they were. And I think this is what God wants of me more than anything else. So I have stopped trying to grow better, and have left myself in His hands to be saved like any other poor sinner. And all I have to do is, just to take the blessings He sends day by day, and they are innumerable, and enjoy them as His gifts, and wait quietly till He takes me out of this lower school and puts me into a higher class in the heavenly home, where I shall learn to love Him as I ought.

"I have written this because it seems to me as though it might help you a little. Friends have told you, I suppose, a hundred times, to just give up all your own efforts and trust in Christ, whether you felt or saw anything or not. I can only repeat that same lesson. You will never be any more fit to trust, than you are to-day. Suppose you knew your life would end this week; would not your instinctive feeling be, 'I can only trust in the Lord?' Well, if you can only rest on Him in like manner now, He will in time make known to you that you are His. Do you suppose any enemy of God was ever distressed as you are because God was not more real? Never! I wish I could tell you some of the sweet thoughts I have had about Jesus visiting the sick when He was upon earth. Have you noticed how much the gospel says about it? And I have thought, if He came to me and healed me, I should want to take Him right to your room and ask Him to heal you. Some day He will. I am as sure of it as I am that it is He who makes me cheerful and happy every day. Can you not trust Him, dear, and wait His time? They tell me that I am an entirely different person since my illness; and I think it is true. It is the Lord's doing. Earthly cares laid aside in a great measure, spiritual burdens dropped at His feet who bids us "let not our hearts be troubled," — I have been quietly waiting through sunshine and shadow for the coming of His messenger. I have enjoyed much this winter. I have no wonderful experiences, no ecstasies, no new views of Christ and His love. I love to live. And God has lavished such countless blessings of every description upon me in these months of my decline, that it has been a perpetual joy to recount them to myself and to those about me. The future seems so full of awe and majesty as to bewilder me; so I do not think much about it; but go trusting along from day to day with a glad heart, knowing that my God will not fail me when the time of trial comes. I have not attained what I have struggled for so many years; but I am one of the Lord's little ones, I hope; and He keeps me so quiet! It sometimes almost seems to me as if I had begun to live in a little piece of heaven already."

To another friend she wrote: "I went to church last Monday afternoon and sat in my own seat for the first time since I returned from E. Perhaps you would hardly have known me with my gay purple wrapper, my S .... shawl and little black velvet bonnet with white velvet flowers. I was told that some 'one had said, "How pretty Mrs. G. looked to-day."' I'm glad of it, if I did, I said, for I tried my best to do so. It would be very foolish to tell you this, were it not that I had this thought in my heart; I wanted to lay off my mourning, and everything that looked gloomy; so that if the people never saw me again, their last memory of me should be a bright and cheerful one; and this not for my own sake either, but because God has done so much for me, and I want everybody to think pleasant thoughts of Him, every time they look at or think of me. It seems as if I had dishonored Him so much by being gloomy in the past, that now I want to make up for it in every way I can. I shall never forget your parlor, dear J., and the spot where I sat on that memorable August 15th. I did not know then what I now see plainly, that the Lord Himself was there also; that He took my hand that day as it were with a new and firmer grasp;

and He has never let it go since. I have felt from that very hour a rest that I did not have before, and I think now it is because I saw plainly then that I had no more time to make myself better; and so I gave myself just as I was, then and there once for all. I had always been a good deal more anxious to grow better than I had been to trust in God. It is a great deal easier to let the Lord save me, than to try to save myself. So I am happy every day. Not because I am so much better than I used to be. But I do trust more; and as to the sins, and neglects, omissions, etc., that used to weigh me down so, why the blood of Christ cleanseth from all sin; and since the Lord has undertaken the work, why not let Him do the whole of it, as well as a part? So every time Satan, or my conscience, says, You sin in this way; or you sinned so and so; I say, I know it; there's no denying that; but 'His blood cleanseth from all sin.' That little word all is such a comfort to me!"

One of our poets has said, "Love hath eyes." The First Commandment warrants and defends this utterance. To love Jesus with all the heart, soul, mind, and strength is to see Him. As is our love so must be the vision.

www.ingramcontent.com/pod-product-compliance
Lightning Source LLC
Chambersburg PA
CBHW031727230426
43669CB00007B/275